PRIMARY MATHEMATICS

Challenging
Word Problems

 **Marshall Cavendish**
Education

 SingaporeMath.com Inc

© 2011 Marshall Cavendish International (Singapore) Private Limited

Published by Marshall Cavendish Education
An imprint of Marshall Cavendish International (Singapore) Private Limited
Times Centre, 1 New Industrial Road, Singapore 536196
Customer Service Hotline: (65) 6411 0820
E-mail: tmesales@sg.marshallcavendish.com
Website: www.marshallcavendish.com/education

First published 2011

Marshall Cavendish is a trademark of Times Publishing Limited.

ISBN 978-981-285-534-3

Printed in Singapore by Times Printers, www.timesprinters.com

Distributed in the U.S.A. by SingaporeMath.com Inc

SingaporeMath.com Inc

The Publisher would like to recognize the contribution of Jennifer Hoerst (Curriculum Advisor,
SingaporeMath.com Inc) to Primary Mathematics Challenging Word Problems.

Preface

 **Challenging Word Problems** provides graded exercises for students of mixed abilities and challenging questions for better math students. This series is written to supplement Singapore's **Primary Mathematics** textbooks, both U.S. and Standards editions, distributed by SingaporeMath.com, Inc. for use in the U.S.A.

Adopting a topical approach in which mathematical concepts and skills are taught and reinforced, the **Challenging Word Problems** series serves to improve students' problem-solving skills and enhance their mathematical reasoning.

Each book in the series features the following:

- **Worked Examples** for each topic show common methods of solution used in the Primary Mathematics textbooks;

- **Practice Questions** allow students to apply and practice questions similar to the ones discussed in the Worked Examples and in the Primary Mathematics textbooks;

- **Challenging Problems** provide opportunities for more capable students to solve higher-order word problems and further develop their problem-solving skills;

- **Mixed Problems** allow students to test their understanding of the concepts discussed in earlier topics and in the Primary Mathematics textbooks;

- **Answers** allow teachers or students to check their answers to all practice exercises and challenging problems;

- **Worked solutions** provide commonly used methods of solving non-routine questions, while encouraging creative or intuitive ones as well.

A student's guide to using the **Challenging Word Problems** series effectively.

1. Read each question given in the Worked Example. Try to solve it before reading the solution.

2. If your solution is similar to the one given in the Worked Example, well done. If you have used a different method, yet have arrived at the same answer, great – you now have at least two methods of solving this question.

3. If your answer is different, look at your work again and figure out where you may have gone wrong.

4. If you have understood all the worked examples, proceed to the Practice Questions; then check your answers with the ones at the back of the book. Should you get stuck at any question, don't panic; go through it again. If you still find difficulty in solving the question, seek help from your friend or teacher.

5. If you have understood and solved all the Practice Questions, you are now ready to try the Challenging Problems. Do them on your own first. Seek help only if you need some hints or clarification.

6. Try to come up with similar questions and challenge your friends to solve them. For a given question, discuss some possible solutions that you may have used in arriving at the answer.

Contents

BLANK

1 Algebra

Worked Example 1

(a) Find the value of $3p + 4q$ when $p = 4$ and $q = 3$.
(b) If $p = 4$ and $3p + 4q = 36$, what is the value of q?

(a) When $p = 4$ and $q = 3$,
$$3p + 4q = (3 \times 4) + (4 \times 3)$$
$$= 12 + 12$$
$$= 24$$

The value of $3p + 4q$ is **24**.

(b) If $p = 4$ and $3p + 4q = 36$,
$$(3 \times 4) + 4q = 36$$
$$12 + 4q = 36$$
$$4q = 36 - 12$$
$$= 24$$
$$q = 24 \div 4$$
$$= 6$$

The value of q is **6**.

Worked Example 2

The average weight of 5 girls is p lbs. If the weight of one girl is 45 lbs, what is the average weight of the remaining girls in terms of p?

Average weight of 5 girls = p lbs
Total weight of all 5 girls = $5 \times p$ lbs
$$= 5p \text{ lbs}$$

One girl weighs 45 lbs.

Total weight of the remaining girls = $(5p - 45)$ lbs

Average weight of the remaining girls = $(\frac{5p - 45}{4})$ lbs

The average weight of the remaining girls is $(\frac{5p - 45}{4})$ **lbs**.

Worked Example 3

Write an expression for the number of
(a) centimeters in p meters.
(b) millimeters in b meters.
(c) kilograms in m grams.

(a) In 1 m, there are 100 cm.
In p m, there are $p \times 100$ cm $= 100p$ cm.

p m = **100p cm**

(b) In 1 m, there are 100 cm.
In 1 cm, there are 10 mm.
In 1 m, there are 100×10 mm $= 1000$ mm.
In b m, there are $b \times 1000$ mm $= 1000b$ mm.

b m = **1000b mm**

(c) There are 1000 g in 1 kg.
1000 g = 1 kg

$$1 \text{ g} = \frac{1}{1000} \text{ kg}$$

$$m \text{ g} = m \times \frac{1}{1000}$$
$$= \frac{m}{1000} \text{ kg}$$

Practice Questions

Answer all questions.

1. If x is a number, write down an expression for a number that is

    (a) 3 more than x.

    (b) 2 less than x.

    (c) 4 times x.

    (d) $\frac{1}{5}$ of x.

2. The product of two numbers is 10. One of the numbers is p. Write down an expression for the other number.

3. Write down an expression for the number of days in a weeks.

4. When x apples were shared among y children, none were left over. Write down an expression for the number of apples each child received.

5. Write down an expression for
   (a) p minutes in hours.
   (b) q days in weeks.

6. The length of a rectangle is a cm and its width is b cm. Write down an expression for
   (a) its perimeter.
   (b) its area.
   Simplify your answers.

7. A bag contains u coins. If v coins are removed from the bag and another w coins are added to the bag, how many coins will there be in the bag in the end?

8. Find the value of x in the equation $8x - 25 = 0$.

9. A van can travel p miles on q gallons of gas. How many gallons of gas will it need to travel r miles?

10. Write an expression for each unknown length m and n in the rectangle below.

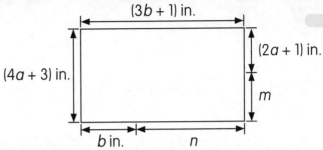

11. What is the largest possible value of $(\dfrac{a+b+c}{d \times e \times f})$ if a, b, c, d, e, and f are different whole numbers from 1 to 9?

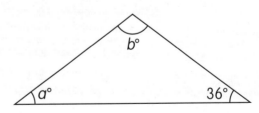

When is the numerator the largest? When is the denominator the smallest?

12. In the figure below, if $b = 3a$, find the values of a and b.

Challenging Problems

Worked Example 1

Lemuel sold 48 notebooks in 3 days. Each day he sold 2 more notebooks than what he had sold the previous day. How many notebooks did he sell each day?

Method 1

Let x be the number of notebooks sold on the first day,
$(x + 2)$ be the number of notebooks sold on the second day, and
$(x + 4)$ be the number of notebooks sold on the third day.

$$x + (x + 2) + (x + 4) = 48$$
$$3x + 6 = 48$$
$$3x = 48 - 6$$
$$= 42$$
$$x = 42 \div 3$$
$$= 14$$

Lemuel sold **14 notebooks on the first day**, **16 notebooks on the second day**, and **18 notebooks on the third day**.

Method 2

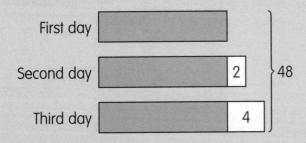

First day

Second day   2

Third day   4   } 48

3 units ⟶ 48 − 2 − 4 = 42
1 unit ⟶ 42 ÷ 3 = 14

Lemuel sold **14 notebooks on the first day**, **16 notebooks on the second day**, and **18 notebooks on the third day**.

Method 3

Since Lemuel sold 48 notebooks in 3 days, he sold an average of 48 ÷ 3 = 16 notebooks each day. This represents the number of notebooks sold on the second day.

Since 2 more notebooks were sold each day than on the previous day, Lemuel sold 16 − 2 = **14 notebooks on the first day**, **16 notebooks on the second day**, and 16 + 2 = **18 notebooks on the third day**.

Check your answer by working backwards.

Worked Example 2

Write an expression for
(a) $(u + v)$ and w cents in cents.
(b) $10k$ meters in centimeters.
(c) 3800 seconds in hours.

(a) In \$1, there are 100¢.
In $(u + v)$, there are $(u + v) \times 100¢ = 100(u + v)¢$.
$100(u + v)¢ + w¢ = [100(u + v) + w]¢$

The number of cents in $(u + v)$ and w cents is **$[100(u + v) + w]$¢**.

(b) In 1 m, there are 100 cm.
In $10k$ m, there are $10k \times 100$ cm $= 1000k$ cm.

The number of centimeters in $10k$ meters is **$1000k$ cm**.

(c) In 1 h, there are 60 min.
In 1 min, there are 60 s.
In 1 h, there are 60×60 s $= 3600$ s.

3600 s $= 1$ h

1 s $= \dfrac{1}{3600}$ h

3800 s $= 3800 \times \dfrac{1}{3600}$ h

$\quad\quad = \dfrac{3800}{3600}$ h

$\quad\quad = 1\dfrac{1}{18}$ h

The number of hours in 3800 seconds is **$1\dfrac{1}{18}$ h**.

Answer all questions.

1. Find the value of n in the equation $5n - 2 = 2n + 10$.

2. If the value of $(52x - 13y)$ is 65, what is the value of $(28x - 7y)$?
   [Hint: $52x - 13y = 13 \times (4x - y)$]

3. The figure below is made up of two squares. The total area of both squares is 136 cm^2. What is the value of $(x + y)$?

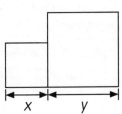

4. Look at the pattern below.

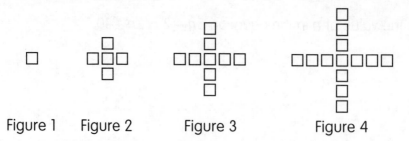

Figure 1   Figure 2   Figure 3   Figure 4

(a) Draw the next figure.
(b) How many cubes are needed for the 7th and 12th figures?
(c) How many cubes are needed for the nth figure? Give your answer in
    terms of n.

5. There were x candies in a bag. Jane took some candies from the bag.
   Ruth took twice as many candies as Jane. Sally took 25 more candies
   than Jane. The bag is now empty.
   (a) Express the number of candies that Jane took in terms of x.
   (b) If $x = 265$, find the number of candies that each girl took.

6. The cost of four items in a cafe is as follows:

Item	Cost
Cup of tea	80¢
Cup of coffee	90¢
Egg sandwich	$1.20
Tuna sandwich	$1.30

Find the cost of each of the following orders.
(a) 2 cups of tea and 2 egg sandwiches
(b) 2 cups of coffee, 1 cup of tea, 2 tuna sandwiches, and 1 egg sandwich
(c) m cups of tea and n cups of coffee
(d) p egg sandwiches and q tuna sandwiches
(e) a cups of tea, b cups of coffee, c egg sandwiches, and d tuna sandwiches

7. Shop P has 210 television sets. It has y fewer television sets than Shop Q. Shop Q has $\frac{1}{3}$ as many television sets as Shop R.

(a) How many more television sets does Shop R have than Shop P?
(b) If $y = 110$, how many television sets do the three shops have in all?

8. There are *w* lamp posts on a road. The distance between each lamp post is 20 ft. If there is a lamp post at the beginning and end of the road, express the length of the road in terms of *w*.

9. There are 30 strips of paper, each of length *x* cm. Each strip overlaps with the end of another strip by 2 cm. If all the strips of paper are glued together to form a longer strip, express the length of the longer strip in terms of *x*.

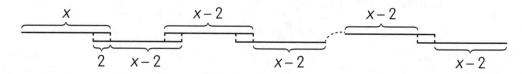

10. An apple costs *p*¢. An orange costs *q*¢ more than an apple. What is the total cost of 2 apples and 3 oranges?

2 Fractions

Worked Example 1

Gerald and Lisa went shopping with a total of $288. Gerald spent $\frac{2}{5}$ of his money and Lisa spent $36. Gerald found that the amount he had left was $\frac{1}{3}$ of the amount Lisa had left. How much did Lisa have at first?

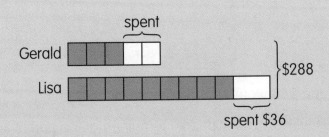

14 units ⟶ $288 − $36 = $252

1 unit ⟶ $252 ÷ 14 = $18

9 units ⟶ 9 × $18 = $162

$162 + $36 = $198

Lisa had **$198** at first.

Practice Questions

Answer all questions.

1. $\frac{3}{5}$ of a number is 18. What is $\frac{7}{10}$ of the number?

2. There were 198 men and 256 women at a party. $\frac{1}{3}$ of the men and $\frac{1}{4}$ of the women left early. How many people remained at the party?

3. String P is $\frac{2}{5}$ ft. long. String Q is $\frac{3}{4}$ ft. longer than String P. String R is $\frac{7}{10}$ ft. shorter than String Q. What is the total length of strings P, Q, and R?

4. Kelvin and 7 of his friends shared $3\frac{1}{5}$ similar packets of pistachio nuts equally. Jane and 6 of her friends shared $2\frac{5}{8}$ similar packets of pistachio nuts equally. Which group had a bigger share each?

5. $\frac{1}{3}$ of the students go to school by bus. $\frac{1}{4}$ of the remaining students go to school by car. The rest of them either ride a bicycle or walk to school. If 90 students go to school by car, how many students are there in the school?

6. Timothy had $\frac{5}{8}$ as many coins as Pearly. After Pearly gave $\frac{1}{4}$ of her coins to Timothy, Timothy had 10 coins more than Pearly. How many coins did Timothy have at first?

7. Esther had five times as many cards as Richard. Esther gave $\frac{1}{4}$ of her cards to Richard. Then, Richard gave $\frac{1}{6}$ of his cards to Esther in return. In the end, Esther had 90 cards more than Richard. How many cards did Esther have at first?

8. Samuel and Jill had 576 stamps in all. Samuel gave $\frac{1}{7}$ of his stamps to Jill. Then, Jill gave $\frac{1}{4}$ of the total number of stamps she now had to Samuel. In the end, both of them had the same number of stamps. What was the difference in the number of stamps they each had at first?

9. $\frac{1}{4}$ of Henry's stickers is equal to $\frac{2}{3}$ of Daisy's stickers. The difference in the number of stickers each of them has is 135. How many stickers do they have in all?

10. Beth and Joanne had $2880 in all. Beth gave $\frac{1}{4}$ of her money to Joanne. Then, Joanne gave $\frac{1}{3}$ of the total amount she had to Beth. In the end, both girls had the same amount of money.
(a) How much did Beth have at first?
(b) How much did Joanne have at first?
(Hint: Work backwards.)

11. One big ball bearing weighs $1\frac{1}{2}$ times as much as a small ball bearing.

Find all the combinations of small and big ball bearings that will be needed to balance 10 small ball bearings.

12. Matthew spent $3000 of his salary on an air conditioner and $\frac{1}{5}$ of his remaining salary on a pair of shoes. If he had $\frac{2}{5}$ of his salary left in the end, how much was his salary?

Challenging Problems

Worked Example 1

Kylie and Faith had 600 seashells in all. After Kylie gave away $\frac{2}{7}$ of her seashells and Faith threw away 120 of her seashells, they had the same number of seashells left. How many seashells did they have left?

Before

Kylie

Faith

} 600

120

After

Kylie

Faith

} ?

12 units ⟶ 600 − 120 = 480
1 unit ⟶ 480 ÷ 12 = 40
10 units ⟶ 10 × 40 = 400

They had **400** seashells left.

Answer all questions.

1. Ann had some stickers. She gave $\frac{1}{2}$ of them to Betty. Then, she gave $\frac{1}{8}$ of what she had left to Sammy. When she met Paul, she gave him $\frac{1}{7}$ of what she had left. Next, she decided to share her remaining stickers equally with Mary. Ann was left with 12 stickers in the end. How many stickers did Ann have at first?

2. Gavin had a sum of money. He gave $\frac{1}{2}$ of it to the African Wildlife Foundation. Then, he gave $\frac{1}{4}$ of what he had left to the American Red Cross. Next, he gave the Mercy Corps $\frac{1}{3}$ of what he had left. Lastly, he donated $\frac{1}{2}$ of what he had to the Global Fund for Women. Gavin was left with $625 in the end. How much money did he have at first?

3. Aquatic plants growing above the surface of a pond cover twice as much of the surface every day, compared to the day before. If the plants cover the surface of the pond completely on the 20th day, on which day was $\frac{1}{4}$ of the surface of the pond covered?

4. Cherie read $\frac{1}{5}$ of a book in 5 days. She read the same number of pages each day. After reading for another 8 days, she had 192 pages left to read.
   (a) What fraction of the book was not read?
   (b) How many pages were there in the book?

5. Jenny had 260 fewer melons than pineapples at her stall. $\frac{2}{3}$ of the number of melons was equal to $\frac{1}{4}$ of the number of pineapples. If all the melons were sold to 6 customers and each customer bought an equal number of melons, how many melons did each customer buy?

6. Mrs. Jones and Claire had a total of $720 in all. After Mrs. Jones had spent $\frac{4}{7}$ of her money and Claire had spent $150, Mrs. Jones found that the amount of money Claire had left was $\frac{5}{6}$ of what she had left. How much money did Claire have at first?

7. The sum of $\frac{1}{4}$ of the number of red balls and $\frac{2}{5}$ of the number of green balls is equal to 21 balls. The sum of $\frac{3}{4}$ of the number of red balls and $\frac{4}{5}$ of the number of green balls is equal to 47 balls. How many red balls and green balls are there?

8. Mrs. Klum withdrew $\frac{1}{8}$ of her savings from her bank account. She used $\frac{4}{7}$ of the money to buy a coffee table. If the coffee table cost $420, how much did she have in her bank account at first?

9. Mrs. Oliver had 400 grapefruits and mangoes. She sold $\frac{3}{4}$ of the grapefruits and $\frac{2}{3}$ of the mangoes. Then she had 120 grapefruits and mangoes left. What fraction of the fruits were mangoes at first?

10. Mr. Perez had 48 more chairs than tables in his furniture store.

    After selling off $\frac{5}{6}$ of the chairs and $\frac{3}{4}$ of the tables, there were 33 chairs and tables left.
    (a) How many tables were there at first?
    (b) What fraction of the items sold were chairs?

3 Percentage

Worked Example 1

In a farm, the number of pigs is twice the number of goats and the number of goats is three times the number of sheep. What percentage of the total number of animals are sheep?

Sheep
Goats
Pigs

10 units ⟶ 100%
  1 unit ⟶ 100% ÷ 10 = 10%

10% of the total number of animals are sheep.

The total number of animals make up 100%.

Worked Example 2

The *Metric Awareness Week* in 1964 was attended by 10,000 people. The 30th anniversary of the *Metric Awareness Week* in 1994 was attended by 1,000,000 people. What percent increase does it represent?

Year	Number of people
1964	10,000
1994	1,000,000

$$\frac{1,000,000 - 10,000}{10,000} \times 100\% = \frac{990,000}{10,000} \times 100\%$$
$$= 9900\%$$

It represents a **9900%** increase.

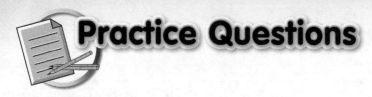

Practice Questions

Answer all questions.

1. Bob earns 50% more than Ruth. How many times of Ruth's earnings is Bob's earnings?

2. The number of chocolate cookies in a box is 25% of the number of other types of cookies. What percentage of the number of cookies are chocolate cookies?

3. The discount on a bag was increased to 7% from 5%. Find the percent increase in the discount.

4. (a) The monthly interest rate at Zimex Bank is 0.1%. How much interest is earned on a $10,000 deposit after a month?

   (b) The monthly interest rate on a $20,000 deposit is $\frac{1}{8}$%. Find the interest earned after a month.

5. The toll for motorists on a new highway rose from $2 to $3. Find the percent increase in the toll.

6. In January, Abigail gets a monthly allowance of $45 from her mother. In February, her mother increases her allowance by 25%. Her mother then decreases her allowance in March by 25%. What is the percent increase or decrease in her allowance in March, as compared to her allowance in January?

7. A bricklayer needs 10,000 bricks to build a house. On average, no more than 7% of a load of bricks are broken on delivery. If bricks are delivered in lots of 100, what is the least number of bricks that he should order so that there are enough bricks to finish building the house? Give your answer to the nearest hundred bricks.

8. There are two written papers for a mathematics exam. Paper 1 has a total score of 80 points and Paper 2 has a total score of 120 points. If Sandra scores 60 points for Paper 1 and 100 points for Paper 2, what is her overall score, expressed as a percentage?

9. Jay claims that an increase of 5% of a number followed by a decrease of 10% is equivalent to a decrease of 10% followed by an increase of 5%. Is he correct? Explain your answer.

10. There are 140 members in a chess club. 75% of the members are boys and the rest are girls. How many percent more boys are there?

11. Corinne, Eileen, and Fiona each have some money. Corinne has 20% less money than Eileen and Fiona has 25% more money than Eileen. Express the amount of money Corinne has as a percentage of the amount of money Fiona has.

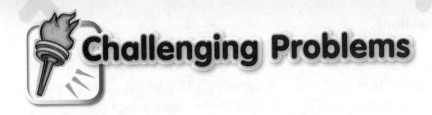

Challenging Problems

Worked Example 1

During a sale, a furniture store advertises that its everyday low prices is 65% off the retail price. On a public holiday, the store advertises that its special holiday prices will be 75% off the retail price. What percentage discount is the store offering off its everyday low prices on the public holiday? Give your answer to the nearest percent.

65% off the retail price means that the store's everyday low prices are 35% of the retail price. On the public holiday, 75% off the retail price means that the prices are 25% of the retail price.
This means that there is a further increase in discount of
35% − 25% = 10%.

$$\frac{10}{35} \times 100\% = 28\frac{4}{7}\%$$
$$\approx 29\%$$

The store is offering about **29%** discount off its everyday low prices on the public holiday.

Answer all questions.

1. A company's sales increased by 10% in 2007, followed by another 20% increase in 2008. Its sales decreased by 20% in 2009, followed by another 10% decrease in 2010. Find the percent increase or decrease in the company's sales from 2007 to 2010.

2. $\frac{2}{3}$ of the students in a class failed a geometry test. 40% of the students who had failed, passed the retest. Find the percentage of students who passed after the retest.

3. During a sale, the price of a radio set was reduced by 20%. After the sale, the price of the radio set was increased back to the original price. By what percent was the sale price increased to restore the original price?

4. Mrs. Parker misplaced 10% of her brooches in May. She misplaced another 10% of her brooches in June but managed to find 10% of the brooches that she misplaced in May. What percentage of her brooches did she have in the end?

5. Jake will earn $2400 if he sells his vintage watch set at a discount of 5% off the usual price. If he sells the watch set at a discount of 25% off the usual price, he will lose $900. What is the cost price of the vintage watch set?

6. There are 60 students in a class. 25% of the students are girls. When more girls join the class, the percentage of girls increases to 40%. How many more girls join the class?

7. 3% of births in a country are twins. What percentage of the newborn babies is made up of twins? 3%, less than 3%, or more than 3%?

8. The water content in 10 lbs of fresh figs was reduced from 99% to 98% after they were dried under the sun. What is the weight of the figs now? (Hint: The solid weight of the figs remains constant.)

9. There were a total of 1200 watches and clocks in a shop, of which 60% were watches. After some watches were sold, the percentage of watches remaining dropped to 20%. How many watches were sold?

10. At a public forum, 60% of the participants were men and the rest were women. When 140 more participants joined in, the number of men increased by 20% and the number of women increased by 40%. How many participants were there at the forum in the end?

Worked Example 1

The ratio of the number of Josh's stamps to Bob's was 4 : 5. After Josh received another 18 stamps from his father, he had twice as many stamps as Bob. How many stamps did Josh have at first?

Before

Josh

Bob

After

received 18 stamps

Josh

Bob

6 units ⟶ 18
1 unit ⟶ 18 ÷ 6 = 3
4 units ⟶ 4 × 3 = 12

Josh had **12** stamps at first.

Worked Example 2

The ratio of the number of Nick's marbles to Michel's is 3 : 5. Nick has 36 marbles. If Nick receives another 9 marbles, what will be the new ratio of the number of Nick's marbles to Michel's?

Before

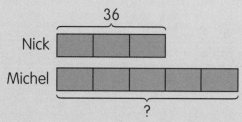

After

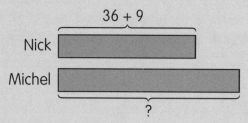

3 units ⟶ 36
1 unit ⟶ 36 ÷ 3 = 12
5 units ⟶ 5 × 12 = 60
Michel has 60 marbles.

36 + 9 = 45
Nick has 45 marbles now.

45 : 60 = 3 : 4
The new ratio of the number of Nick's marbles to Michel's is **3 : 4**.

Worked Example 3

Joseph had the same amount of money as Martha. After Joseph spent $36 and Martha spent $12, the ratio of the amount of money Joseph had to the amount of money Martha had was 1 : 4. How much money did each of them have at first?

Before

Joseph

Martha

After

$36

Joseph

Martha $12

3 units ⟶ $36 − $12 = $24
1 unit ⟶ $24 ÷ 3 = $8

$8 + $36 = $44

Each of them had **$44** at first.

Practice Questions

Answer all questions.

1. The ratio of the number of Mary's stickers to Anne's is 4 : 7. Mary has
    48 stickers. If Mary buys another 8 stickers, what will be the new ratio
    of the number of Mary's stickers to Anne's?

2. Richard had the same number of bookmarks as Rose. After Richard
    gave away 28 bookmarks and Rose threw away 16 bookmarks, the ratio
    of the number of Richard's bookmarks to Rose's was 2 : 5. How many
    bookmarks did they have in all at first?

3. Anthony has $\frac{4}{7}$ as many stamps as Samson. If Anthony gives $\frac{3}{8}$ of his
    stamps to Samson, what will be the ratio of the number of Anthony's
    stamps to Samson's?

4. The ratio of the number of Chinese books to the number of English books in a bookshop was 4 : 5. After the shop owner bought another 30 Chinese books, there were twice as many Chinese books as English books. How many English books were there?

5. Elizabeth and Paul were paid a sum of $60 to clean a house. The amount was shared between them based on the number of hours each of them worked. Paul started cleaning at 7:00 a.m. and Elizabeth only joined him at 9:00 a.m. They finished cleaning the house at 1:00 p.m. How much was each of them paid?

6. The ratio of the number of Karen's dolls to Hannah's was 8 : 3. After Karen gave 15 dolls to Hannah, they each had the same number of dolls. How many dolls did Karen have at first?

7. Some biscuits are shared between David and Nicholas in the ratio 6 : 5. The ratio of the number of Nicholas's biscuits to Fiona's is 7 : 10. If David has 8 biscuits fewer than Fiona, how many biscuits does Nicholas have?

8. The ratio of the number of Claude's books to Robin's is 5 : 6. The ratio of the number of Robin's books to Ian's is 7 : 4. If Claude has 22 books more than Ian, how many books does Robin have?

9. The ratio of the amount of money Jim had to the amount of money Chris had was 7 : 10. After Jim spent $27, the ratio of the amount of money Jim had to the amount of money Chris had became 1 : 4. How much money did they have left?

10. The ratio of the number of girls to the number of boys in a classroom was 6 : 5. After 16 girls left the room, the ratio became 2 : 3. How many girls were there at first?

11. Daisy saved $66 while Oliver saved $82. Each of them donated the same amount of money to a charity. Then, the ratio of Daisy's savings to Oliver's savings became 3 : 7.
    (a) How much savings did they have left?
    (b) How much money did each of them donate?

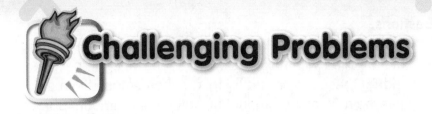

Challenging Problems

Worked Example 1

The ratio of Sue's mother's age to Sue's age is 2 : 1. If their combined age is 63 years, what will be their combined age when Sue reaches the current age of her mother?

Method 1

<u>Now</u>

Sue

Sue's mother } 63

<u>Later</u>

Sue

Sue's mother } ?

3 units ⟶ 63
1 unit ⟶ 63 ÷ 3 = 21
5 units ⟶ 5 × 21 = 105

Their combined age will be **105 years**.

Method 2

If Sue is x years old now, then her mother must be $2x$ years old now.

$3x = 63$
$x = 63 ÷ 3$
$= 21$

Sue is currently 21 years old and her mother is 42 years old.

Sue will be $2 × 21 = 42$ years old and her mother will be 63 years old 21 years later.

Their combined age will be $63 + 42 = $ **105 years**.

Answer all questions.

1. Two identical jars are filled with mixtures of water and vinegar in the ratio 1 : 2 and 1 : 3 respectively. Both jars are then emptied into a container. What is the ratio of the amount of water to the amount of vinegar in the resulting mixture?

2. If 3 printers can print 3 pages in 3 seconds, how many pages will 300 similar printers print in 300 seconds?

3. Albert has a number of nickels and dimes. The ratio of the number of nickels to the number of dimes is 2 : 3. After receiving some nickels and dimes from his parents, the ratio becomes 1 : 3. From eighteen nickels at first, the total value of his nickels is now $1. How many dimes did he receive?

4. Among those who voted in an election, the ratio of the number of male voters to the number of female voters was 17 : 15. The ratio would have been 8 : 7 if 90 fewer male voters and 80 fewer female voters had taken part. How many people voted in the election?

5. Town P has $\frac{2}{5}$ as many residents as Town Q. The ratio of the number of residents in Town R to those in Town P is 4 : 7. Town Q has 8100 more residents than Town R. How many residents are there in Town R?

6. If Cecilia gives Edison $60, the ratio of the amount of money Cecilia has to the amount of money Edison has will be 3 : 5. If Edison gives Cecilia $40, he will have the same amount of money as her. How much money did Edison have at first?

7. An egg seller placed some eggs in baskets P, Q, and R in the ratio 4 : 2 : 3. Eggs were taken out of baskets P and Q in the ratio 4 : 1 and then placed in Basket R. As a result, the number of eggs left in baskets P and Q were 48 and 32 respectively. How many eggs were there in Basket R in the end?

8. Candle A and Candle B are lit at the same time. Candle A lasts 9 hours while Candle B lasts 6 hours. Two hours later, the height of the two candles are the same. Find the ratio of the original length of Candle X to Candle Y's.

9. The ratio of the amount of money Henry had to the amount of money Lily had was 3 : 2. After Henry gave away $5 and Lily received $8, the ratio became 5 : 4. How much money did Lily have at first?

10. Sam had some quarters and dimes in the ratio 4 : 7. After exchanging eight quarters for dimes, the ratio of the number of quarters to the number of dimes became 2 : 12. How much money did Sam have?

5 Speed

Worked Example 1

Town X and Town Y are 825 km apart. Christen drives from Town X to Town Y at 65 km/h. At the same time, Penelope drives from Town Y to Town X at 75 km/h. How far apart will they be after 3 hours?

Distance traveled by Christen in 3 h = 3 × 65
= 195 km

Distance traveled by Penelope in 3 h = 3 × 75
= 225 km

825 km – 195 km – 225 km = 405 km

They will be **405 km** apart after 3 hours.

Worked Example 2

Driver A covers only 160 mi using the same amount of time taken by Driver B who covers 240 mi and is traveling 40 mph faster than Driver A. How long does each driver take to complete the journey? Assume that both drivers start traveling at the same time.

Since Driver B travels 40 mph faster than Driver A, this means that for each hour, Driver B will travel 40 mi more than Driver A.

Driver B travels 240 mi – 160 mi = 80 mi more than Driver A.

This distance can be covered in 80 ÷ 40 = 2 h.

Each motorist takes **2 h** to complete the journey.

Practice Questions

Answer all questions.

1. Zachary and Dylan, starting from the same point, walk in opposite directions. Zachary walks at a rate of 8 km/h, and Dylan walks at a rate of 11 km/h. How far apart will they be after $4\frac{1}{2}$ h?

2. Isabella will take 2 h to reach her destination if she drives at a speed of 55 mph. If she drives at 50 mph instead, how much longer will it take her to reach her destination?

3. Car M and Car N are traveling, from opposite directions in different lanes on a freeway, at speeds of 50 km/h and 80 km/h respectively. How far apart are the cars 2 minutes before they pass each other?

4. A truck travels 75 mi in the time that a car travels 100 mi. The car is traveling at 15 mph faster than the truck. What is the speed of the car? Assume that both drivers start at the same time.

5. Two buses are traveling towards each other along a freeway at 60 km/h. If the buses are 30 km apart, how long will it take for them to meet?

6. Tyler and Ava travel along the same route to a distant town. Ava leaves 2 h ahead of Tyler and travels at 60 km/h. Tyler travels at 90 km/h. How long will it take Tyler to overtake Ava?

7. Telephone poles are placed 60 m apart along a highway. If Mr. Tan drives past 24 poles in one minute as he travels along the highway, what is his speed in kilometers per hour?

8. Wyatt plans to travel at a speed of 80 km/h and stop to rest for only 45 min. How long will it take him to complete a 220-km journey?

9. A car traveling at 80 km/h is 2 km behind a van traveling at 70 km/h in the same direction. How long will it take the car to overtake the van?

10. Paul drove at 50 mph and arrived home one hour earlier than he would have if he had driven at 40 mph. How far did he drive?

11. The average speed of a cyclist is p km/h and his walking speed is t km/h.
    (a) What is the time needed for him to cycle q km? Give your answer in terms of p.
    (b) If he walks for 3 h and cycles for 5 h, what is the total distance traveled? Give your answer in terms of p and t.

Challenging Problems

Worked Example 1

A freeway connects Town P to Town Q. A gas station is situated along the freeway such that the distance from Town P to the gas station is twice the distance from Town Q to the gas station. A bus leaves Town Q at 9:00 a.m. and reaches the gas station one hour later. A car leaving Town P and traveling three times faster than the bus has to reach the gas station at the same time as the bus. At what time should the car leave Town P?

Method 1

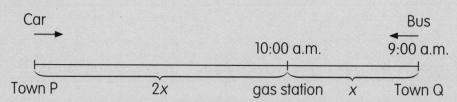

Let the distance from the gas station to Town Q be x km and the distance from the gas station to Town P be $2x$ km.

Since the bus takes 1 h to reach the gas station, let the speed of the bus be x km/h and the speed of the car be $3x$ km/h.

Time taken by the car to reach the station at 10:00 a.m.

$= \dfrac{2x}{3x}$

$= \dfrac{2}{3}$ h

$= 40$ min

The car should leave Town P at **9:20 a.m.**

Method 2

The car travels three times faster than the bus, so the car will take only one-third of the time taken by the bus to cover a certain distance.

The car will take only $\frac{1}{3} \times 1\,h = 20$ min to travel the distance covered by the bus.

But the distance traveled by the car is twice the distance traveled by the bus, so the car will take 2×20 min = 40 min to reach the gas station.

The car should leave Town P at **9:20 a.m.**

Answer all questions.

1. Nathaniel and Trevor each jogged from Park E to Park F. Nathaniel took 2 h to cover the entire journey and Trevor took 1 h to cover three-fifths of the journey. Find the ratio of Nathaniel's average speed to Trevor's average speed.

2. A 100-m long train traveling at a speed of 100 m/s enters a 100-m long tunnel. How long will it take the train to pass completely through the tunnel?

3. Seth and Avery are running in a 100-m race. When Seth crosses the finish line, Avery is only at the 90-m mark. Both of them race against each other again. This time, Seth starts 10 m behind the starting line. Who will win the second race if they each run at the same average speed they ran in the first race?

4. Mackenzie took $7\frac{1}{10}$ h to travel 470 km from Town A to Town B.

   After driving a part of the journey at an average speed of 60 km/h, she stopped for lunch. Then she took another 4 h to complete the remaining part of the journey at an average speed of 80 km/h. Find the length of time she took to have lunch. Give your answer in minutes.

5. Town P and Town Q were 270 mi apart. Charles drove from Town P to Town Q at 9:00 a.m. Timothy drove from Town Q to Town P at 10:00 a.m. Timothy's average speed was 3 times Charles's average speed. They passed each other at noon. What were Charles's and Timothy's average speeds in miles per hour?

6. Luis walked around a circular track once while Arianna ran four times around it in the same direction. Both started from the same point at the same time and returned to that point at the same time. Arianna passed by Luis twice while running. How many times will Arianna pass by Luis if she runs around the track in the opposite direction instead? Assume that Luis's and Arianna's speeds remained the same throughout.

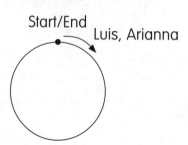

Start/End

Luis, Arianna

7. Gabrielle and Paige drove from Town S to Town T at the same time. They took the same amount of time to complete the journey. Gabrielle spent one-sixth of Paige's traveling time resting, and Paige spent one-fifth of Gabrielle's traveling time resting during the journey. Find the ratio of Gabrielle's speed to Paige's.

8. A driver drove from Town A to Town B at a certain speed. On his way back, he traveled 10 km/h faster and took 12.5% less time to complete the journey. Find the speed the driver traveled at while driving from Town A to Town B.

9. Car S left Town X for Town Y at 7:00 a.m. Car T left Town Y for Town X at the same time. The two cars passed each other at 3:00 p.m. Five hours later, Car S reached Town Y but Car T was still 150 km away from Town X. What was the distance between Town X and Town Y?

10. Carter, Ian, and Jaden walked at a speed of 36 m/min, 42 m/min, and 48 m/min respectively. Carter and Ian started walking from Village X to Village Y at the same time while Jaden walked from Village Y to Village X. Jaden passed by Carter 10 min after passing Ian. Find the distance between the two villages. Give your answer in kilometers.

6 Circles

Worked Example 1

The figure below shows a semicircle in a square. What is the area of the shaded part? (Take $\pi = 3.14$)

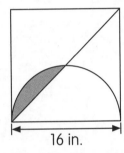

16 in.

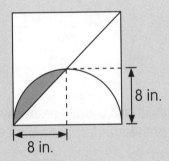

8 in.

8 in.

Area of shaded part = area of quarter circle − area of triangle

$$= \frac{1}{4}\pi r^2 - \frac{1}{2}bh$$

$$= (\frac{1}{4} \times 3.14 \times 8 \text{ in.} \times 8 \text{ in.}) - (\frac{1}{2} \times 8 \text{ in.} \times 8 \text{ in.})$$

$$= 50.24 \text{ in.}^2 - 32 \text{ in.}^2$$

$$= 18.24 \text{ in.}^2$$

The area of the shaded part is **18.24 in.²**.

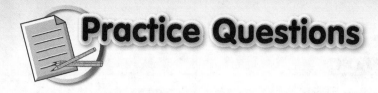

Practice Questions

Answer all questions.

1. The figure below shows a circle in a square. The area of the square is 36 cm². Find the area of the circle. Give your answer in terms of π.

2. The radii of the small and big circles are 2 units and 3 units respectively. Find the area of the shaded part. Give your answer in terms of π.

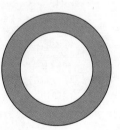

3. A circular swimming pool is surrounded by a 2-m wide pathway.
    The radius of the pool is 16 m. What is the area of the pathway?
    Give your answer in terms of π.

4. The figure below shows three circular pulleys, each of radius 7 cm,
    enclosed within a conveyor belt. Find the length of belt needed to
    enclose the pulleys. (Take $\pi = \frac{22}{7}$)

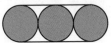

5. OAD is a quarter circle. Its radius is 7 cm. If the shaded part OBEC is a square, what is the length of BC? (Take π = 3.14)

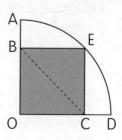

6. What is the greatest possible area of a triangle that can be drawn in a semicircle whose radius is 7 cm?

7. The figure below is made up of 2 identical rectangles and 3 identical semicircles. The radius of the semicircle is 7 cm. What is the area of the figure?

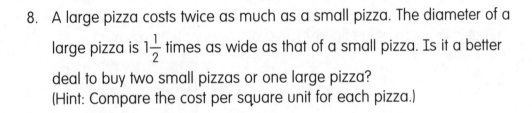

8. A large pizza costs twice as much as a small pizza. The diameter of a large pizza is $1\frac{1}{2}$ times as wide as that of a small pizza. Is it a better deal to buy two small pizzas or one large pizza?
    (Hint: Compare the cost per square unit for each pizza.)

9. The figure below shows 6 circles, each of radius 3 cm, in a rectangle. What is the area of the shaded part? Give your answer in terms of π.

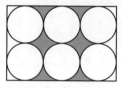

10. The figure below shows a 2-cm square and a three-quarter circle cut out from a 9-cm square. The radius of each quarter circle is 2 cm. What is the area of the figure? Give your answer in terms of π.

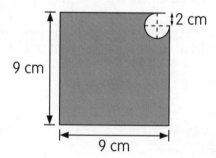

9 cm

9 cm

2 cm

Challenging Problems

Worked Example 1

In the figure below, the four leaves are formed from four semicircles whose diameters are the sides of a square. What is the area of the shaded part?
(Take $\pi = \frac{22}{7}$)

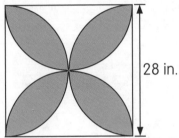

28 in.

Observe that the area of 4 semicircles = area of square + area of 4 leaves (shaded part).

Area of shaded part = area of 4 semicircles − area of square

$$= (4 \times \frac{1}{2} \times \frac{22}{7} \times 14 \text{ in.} \times 14 \text{ in.}) - (28 \text{ in.} \times 28 \text{ in.})$$
$$= 1232 \text{ in.}^2 - 784 \text{ in.}^2$$
$$= 448 \text{ in.}^2$$

The area of the shaded part is **448 in.²**.

Answer all questions.

1. Two wheels with the same diameter are placed next to each other. The position of one wheel is fixed while the second wheel revolves around the fixed wheel. How many complete turns does the second wheel make after moving one complete turn around the fixed wheel?

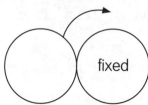

fixed

2. The figure below shows a circle. O is the centre of the circle. What fraction of the circle is shaded? Give your answer in terms of π.

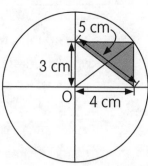

5 cm
3 cm
O
4 cm

3. The figure below shows two similar small circles in a big circle. The radius of the big circle is 1 cm. What fraction of the big circle is shaded?

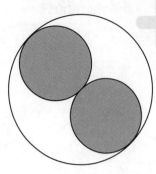

4. The figure below shows three paper cups, each of radius 7 in., placed in a tray. What is the perimeter of the tray? (Take $\pi = \frac{22}{7}$)

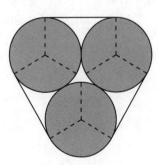

5. A square is drawn inside a circle. O is the center of the circle.
    A rhombus is drawn inside the square. What is the perimeter of
    the rhombus?

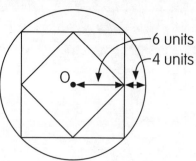

6 units

4 units

6. The figure below shows a square of side 50 cm. What is the total area
    of the shaded parts?

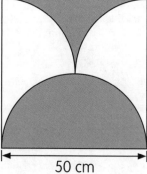

50 cm

7. The figure below is made up of a square and three quarter circles. What is the area of the shaded part?

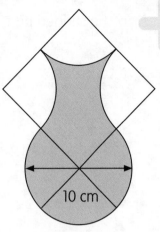

10 cm

8. The figure below shows two quarter circles and two semicircles at the sides of a rectangle. The length of the rectangle is 21 cm. Its width is 14 cm. Find the area and perimeter of the figure. (Take $\pi = \frac{22}{7}$)

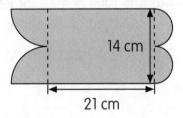

14 cm

21 cm

9. The figure below shows a semicircle of diameter 14 m and two quarter circles, ABC and ABD, in a square. Find the difference between the area of the shaded part X and the shaded part Y. (Take $\pi = \frac{22}{7}$)

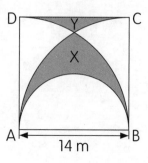

10. The ratio of the diameter of Circle P to the diameter of Circle Q is 1 : 8. The area of the shaded part is 9702 cm². What is the difference in the circumference of the two circles? (Take $\pi = \frac{22}{7}$)

7 Volume

Worked Example 1

A solid wooden cylinder of diameter 28 cm and height 18 cm is placed on the floor. A portion is sawed off by cutting vertically downwards along the radii OA and OB. If the volume of the portion sawed off is $\frac{1}{5}$ of the volume of the wooden cylinder, what is the volume of the remaining solid? (Take $\pi = \frac{22}{7}$)

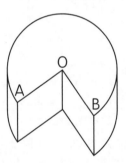

Volume of wooden cylinder $= \pi r^2 h$

$$= \frac{22}{7} \times 14 \text{ cm} \times 14 \text{ cm} \times 18 \text{ cm}$$

$$= 11{,}088 \text{ cm}^3$$

Volume of remaining solid $= (1 - \frac{1}{5}) \times 11{,}088 \text{ cm}^3$

$$= \frac{4}{5} \times 11{,}088 \text{ cm}^3$$

$$= 8870.4 \text{ cm}^3$$

The volume of the remaining solid is **8870.4 cm³**.

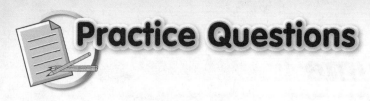

Practice Questions

Answer all questions.

1. Eve used a 12-cm³ glass to pour sand into a container. Adam used a 15-cm³ glass to pour sand into the same container. They stopped pouring in sand when each had poured the same volume of sand into the container.
    (a) Find the number of glasses of sand each had poured into the container.
    (b) What was the volume of sand in the container?

2. A rectangular Container X is completely filled with water. Water in Container X is then used to fill an empty rectangular Container Y to its brim. Container X becomes $\frac{2}{5}$-filled with water. What was the volume of water in Container X at first?

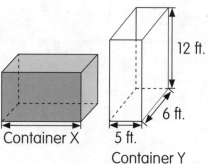

Container X   5 ft.
Container Y

12 ft.

6 ft.

3. One plastic container and two bottles can hold 960 ml of liquid detergent in all. One bottle and two plastic containers can hold 870 ml of liquid detergent in all. Find the capacity of
   (a) one bottle.
   (b) one plastic container.

4. Two square holes, of sides 2 m and 3 m, are drilled through a rectangular wooden block measuring 15 m by 9 m by 6 m. What is the volume of the remaining wooden block?

6 m

15 m

9 m

5. Find the volume of each prism.

(a)

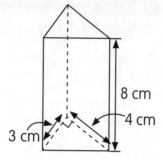

8 cm
4 cm
3 cm

(b)

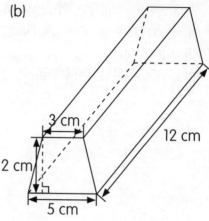

3 cm
12 cm
2 cm
5 cm

6. A horizontal drinking trough has a semicircular cross section. How much water can it hold when full? Give your answer in cubic centimeters.

(Take $\pi = \frac{22}{7}$)

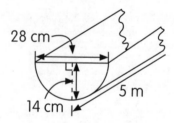

28 cm
14 cm
5 m

7. Water flows at 3 *l* per second through a pipe. Find the time taken to fill up a tank measuring 5 m by 3 m by 2 m. Give your answer correct to the nearest minute.

8. A metal dumbbell has a 3 in. thick wheel, of radius 4 in., attached to each end of a rod. The diameter and length of the rod is 2 in. and 8 in. respectively. Find the volume of the metal dumbbell. (Take π = 3.14)

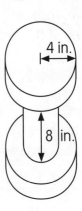

9. A rectangular tank, 24 ft. long and 20 ft. wide, is filled with water to a height of 16 ft. When a metal cube of edge 12 ft. is placed in the tank, the water level rises. What is the new height of the water level?

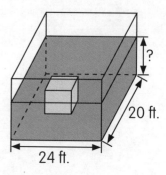

10. A rectangular container, 60 cm long and 20 cm wide, was $\frac{2}{5}$-filled with water. When 11.4 l of water was poured into the container, the water level rose to a height of 23.9 cm. What was the height of the container? (1 l = 1000 cm³)

Challenging Problems

Worked Example 1

A rectangular tank, measuring 45 in. by 30 in. by 48 in., was $\frac{2}{3}$-filled with water. When a stone was placed in the tank, the tank became $\frac{3}{4}$-full. What was the volume of the stone?

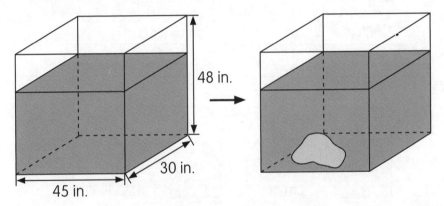

$$\frac{3}{4} - \frac{2}{3} = \frac{9}{12} - \frac{8}{12}$$

$$= \frac{1}{12}$$

$\frac{1}{12}$ of the volume of water in the tank is equal to the volume of the stone.

Volume of stone $= \frac{1}{12} \times 45$ in. $\times 30$ in. $\times 48$ in.

$\qquad\qquad\quad = 5400$ in.^{3}

The volume of the stone was **5400 in.^{3}**.

Answer all questions.

1. Container P is $\frac{2}{3}$-filled with water. Water is then poured from Container P into an empty Container Q until the water levels in both containers are the same. Find the height of the water level in each container.

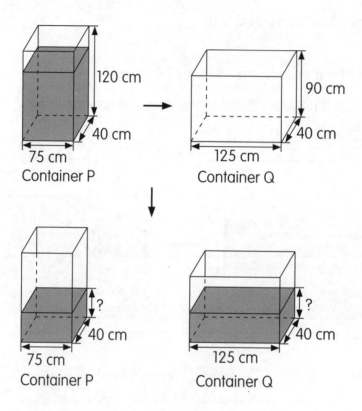

120 cm

40 cm

75 cm

Container P

90 cm

40 cm

125 cm

Container Q

?

40 cm

75 cm

Container P

?

40 cm

125 cm

Container Q

2. When 30 cm³ of water is poured from Tank Q to Tank P, the volume of water in Tank Q becomes 4 times the volume of water in Tank P. When 50 cm³ of water is poured from Tank Q to Tank P, the volume of water in Tank Q then becomes 3 times the volume of water in Tank P. What is the volume of water in Tank Q now?

3. Bottles A and B each contain a different volume of water. $\frac{1}{4}$ of the water in Bottle A is poured into Bottle B. Then, $\frac{1}{4}$ of the water in Bottle B is poured into Bottle A. Now, the two bottles each have the same volume of water. What is the ratio of the initial volume of water in Bottle A to the initial volume of water in Bottle B?

4. The figure below shows a solid made up of two cubes, Cube A and Cube B. The volume of Cube A is 512 cm³. What is the volume of the solid?

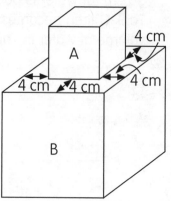

5. The figure below shows part of a gadget. All the corners are square corners and the cross section of the curved surface is a semicircle of diameter 20 cm. What is the volume of the figure? (Take π = 3.14)

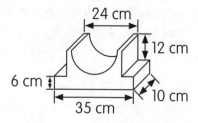

6. Water flows at 2.5 m³ per minute through a pipe. The water is collected in an empty cylindrical tank with an internal diameter of 84 cm. What is the height of the water level in the tank after one minute? Give your answer to the nearest centimeter. (Take $\pi = \frac{22}{7}$)

7. An empty rectangular tank is 60 cm long, 35 cm wide, and 45 cm high. A stone of volume 7500 cm³ is placed in the tank. Water flowing from a tap fills the tank at a rate of 12 l per minute. How long will it take to fill the tank to its brim? (1 l = 1000 cm³)

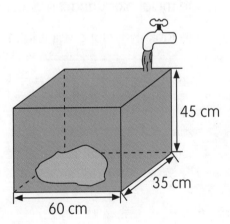

45 cm

35 cm

60 cm

8. A solid is put in an empty rectangular tank that is 60 cm long and 40 cm wide. The tank is then filled with water flowing from a tap at a rate of 9 l per minute. If it takes 3.5 min to fill the tank with water to a height of 24 cm so as to cover the solid completely, what is the volume of the solid? (1 l = 1000 cm^3)

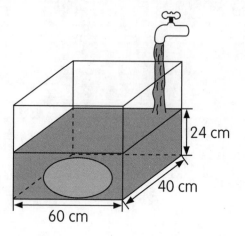

9. A metal block has a volume of 196 cm^3. It is placed in a rectangular tank measuring 12 cm by 15 cm by 18 cm. A tap takes 11 min to fill the tank with just enough water to cover the metal block. The total volume of the metal block and the water in the tank makes up $\frac{2}{5}$ of the capacity of the tank. How long will it take to fill the tank completely?

10. Tap P and Tap Q are used to fill a container, measuring 80 cm by 60 cm by 30 cm, to its brim with water. If only Tap P is turned on, the container will be filled in 8 min. If only Tap Q is turned on, the tank will be filled in 12 min.

(a) If both taps are turned on, what is the total rate of water flowing into the container? Give your answer in liters per minute.

(b) If both taps are turned on at the same time, how long will it take for them to fill the container with water?

8 Data Analysis

Worked Example 1

There are 3 types of fishes in an aquarium. The pie chart represents the number of each type of fish in the aquarium. There are equal numbers of goldfish and angelfish.

(a) What fraction of the fishes in the aquarium are goldfish?

(b) There are 15 angelfish. How many guppies are there in the aquarium?

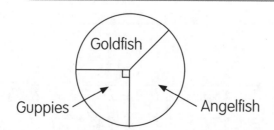

(a) The guppies represent $\frac{90}{360} = \frac{1}{4}$ of the pie chart.

So, the goldfish and angelfish represent $1 - \frac{1}{4} = \frac{3}{4}$ of the pie chart.

The goldfish represent $\frac{1}{2} \times \frac{3}{4} = \frac{3}{8}$ of the fishes in the aquarium.

(b) The angelfish represents $\frac{3}{8}$ of the pie chart.

$\frac{3}{8}$ of the pie chart represents 15 fish.

$\frac{1}{8}$ of the pie chart represents $15 \div 3 = 5$ fish.

$\frac{2}{8}$ of the pie chart represents $2 \times 5 = 10$ fish.

There are **10** guppies in the aquarium.

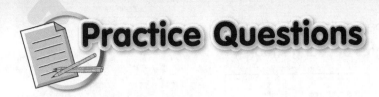

Practice Questions

Answer all questions.

1. The table shows the times taken by 5 runners to complete a race.

Runner	Time taken (in s)
Alvin	15.7
Bobby	15.8
Carl	14.4
Dave	14.3
Emmanuel	15.2

(a) Who came in first in the race?
(b) Who came in last in the race?
(c) What is the range of the time taken by the runners?
(d) What is the mean time taken by the 5 runners?

2. The graph shows the heights of 5 young shoots.

Heights of young shoots

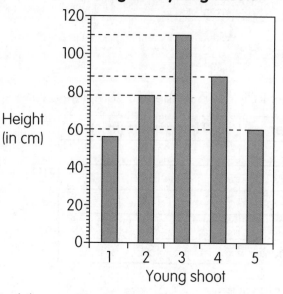

The median of a data set is the middle value when the data are arranged in order.

Find the median height of the young shoots.

3. The table shows the Pollutant Standards Index (PSI) reading taken regularly at noon over a period of 2 weeks.

PSI reading						
30	85	10	40	25	60	55
65	50	70	45	15	20	35

Find the median PSI reading from the data in the table.

4. The pie chart shows the age groups of 120 members in a chess club. What is the median age of the members?

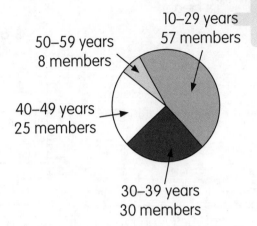

50–59 years
8 members

10–29 years
57 members

40–49 years
25 members

30–39 years
30 members

5. The table shows the scores of a basketball team for eight matches.

Match	1	2	3	4	5	6	7	8
Score	72	51	85	92	64	79	80	68

Find the range of scores.

6. The height of a plant was measured every Friday over a period of
    5 weeks. The line graph shows the growth of the plant with respect to
    its height.

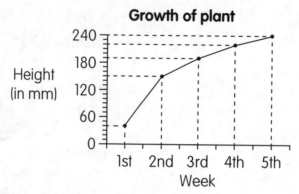

Growth of plant

(a) Between the 2nd and 4th week, what was the mean growth of the
     plant each day?

(b) Find the mean growth of the plant over the 5 weeks.

7. The table shows Alvin's Math test scores during a semester.

Test	1	2	3	4	5	6	7	8
Score	73	69	87	81	69	70	90	69

The mode is the value that occurs most frequently.

Find the
(a) mode.   (b) median score.   (c) mean score.

8. The table shows the toll collected in June along a certain highway.

Toll collected in June					
$2080	$3400	$1950	$2500	$1600	$2100
$2200	$1730	$2750	$3020	$4600	$3000
$3160	$2650	$3350	$1880	$2180	$1980
$2000	$2080	$2810	$2170	$1840	$2300
$3090	$2930	$3140	$2220	$2380	$3260

(a) Find the mean toll collected along the highway in June.
(b) A random sample of 5 days was selected. The toll collected on those days were $1950, $1600, $1730, $1880, and $1840. Find the mean toll collected in this sample.

9. Noah spends half of a school day in school and on homework. The amount of time he spends traveling is the same as the amount of time he spends doing homework. The pie chart represents how Noah spends his time on each school day.

(a) How long does Noah spend in school?

(b) What fraction of his time does he spend traveling?

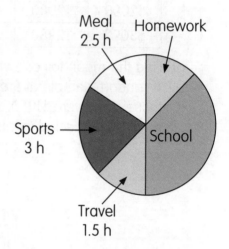

Meal
2.5 h

Homework

Sports
3 h

School

Travel
1.5 h

10. At a fun fair, a group of 60 students sold some T-shirts to raise funds for a charity organization. The table and graph shows the amount of money raised by the students.

Amount of money collected	$20	$25	$30	$35	$40	$45	$50	$55
Number of students	3	6	13	17	12	4	2	3

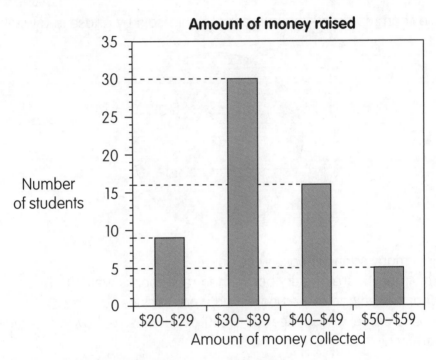

Amount of money raised

Find the median amount of money collected
(a) using the data in the table.
(b) from the data shown in the graph.

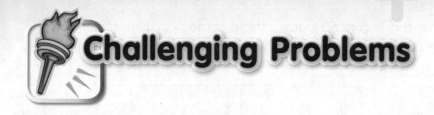

Challenging Problems

Worked Example 1

The pie chart represents the number of books sold by Chase in a week.

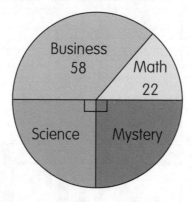

(a) How many science books were sold?
(b) How many more mystery books than math books were sold?
(c) What percentage of the books sold were business books?
(d) If on average, Chase received $4.50 per book sold, how much did he earn in all?

(a) 58 business books + 22 math books represent $\frac{1}{2}$ of the pie chart.

58 + 22 = 80

$\frac{1}{2}$ of the pie chart represents 80 books.

$\frac{1}{4}$ of the pie chart represents 80 ÷ 2 = 40 books.

40 science books were sold.

(b) Mystery books represent $\frac{1}{4}$ of the pie chart.

So, 40 mystery books were sold.
40 – 22 = 18

40 – 22 = **18** more mystery books than math books were sold.

(c) Total number of books sold = 4 × 40
$$= 160$$
$$\frac{58}{160} \times 100\% = 36.25\%$$

36.25% of the books sold were business books.

(d) 160 × \$4.50 = \$720

He earned **\$720** in all.

Answer all questions.

1. Study the two groups of data.

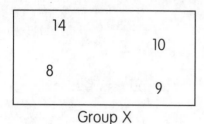

Group X

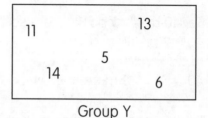

Group Y

Which number from Group X must be switched with another number from Group Y so that both groups will have the same mean?

2. In the given set of numbers, p and q represent whole numbers. The mean and median are also whole numbers.

   10   7   9   12   6 p q

   For what values of p and q would the mean and the median be the same?

3. I am thinking of 6 different odd numbers.
   The mean of the numbers is 16.
   The median is 15.
   The range is 26.
   The greatest number is 31.
   What is the greatest possible value for the second number?

4. Each set of six whole numbers has a mean of 4.

Set 1:	1	2	3	4	5	9
Set 2:	1	2	3	5	6	7
Set 3:	1	1	1	1	2	18
Set 4:	3	4	4	4	4	5

Find another three sets of six whole numbers which have a mean of 4 each.

5. The table shows the earnings of 24 cab drivers on Monday.

Earnings				
$110	$130	$103	$95	$130
$83	$120	$117	$97	$124
$121	$87	$123	$101	$110
$135	$85	$145	$123	$88
$92	$102	$132	$117	

(a) Find the median earnings.
(b) Another cab driver's earnings of $100 is added to the data set. Find the new median earnings.

6. The pie chart represents the total number of people who attended a computer fair.

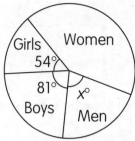

(a) What percentage of the people who attended the computer fair were girls?

(b) If there were twice as many women as men, find the value of x.

(c) If there were 324 girls, how many people attended the computer fair?

7. The line graph shows the number of hours Jeremiah, Erin, and Carlos worked from January to September.

(a) Find the average number of hours that Jeremiah, Erin, and Carlos worked from April to June? Give your answer correct to the nearest hour.

(b) In July, Carlos was paid $5 per hour for the first 100 hours and $8 per hour for the subsequent hours. Jeremiah was paid $7 per hour for the first 75 hours and $9 per hour for the subsequent hours. Erin was paid $6 per hour for the first 65 hours and $8 per hour for the subsequent hours. Find their average wage in July. Give your answer to the nearest dollar.

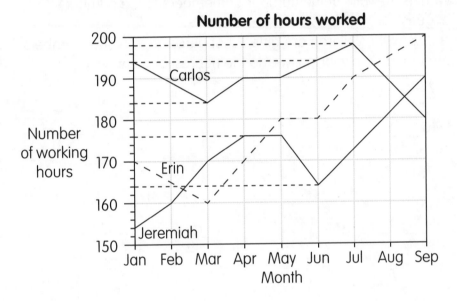

Number of hours worked

8. The pie chart represents a total of 2400 people at a country club.

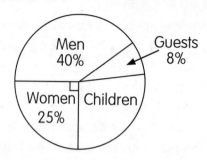

(a) Find the number of children at the country club.
(b) What is the ratio of the number of members to the number of guests?
(c) If 25% of the children are girls, what percentage of the members are male? Give your answer to the nearest percent.

9. The graph shows the weights of eleven aquariums on display in a shop.

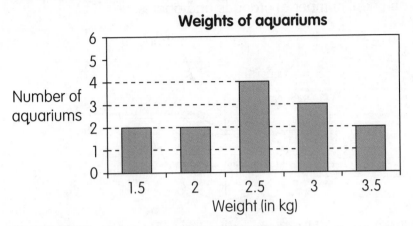

Weights of aquariums

Number of aquariums (vertical axis)

Weight (in kg) (horizontal axis)

(a) Find the mean weight of the aquariums.
(b) Find the median weight of the aquariums.
(c) Five more aquariums weighing 2 kg, 2 kg, 3 kg, 3.5 kg, and 3.5 kg are put on display. What is the new mean and median weight of the aquariums?

10. The pie chart represents the number of fruits sold by a fruit seller in May. He sold an equal number of oranges and apples.

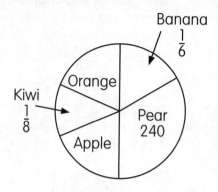

(a) Find the number of bananas sold.

(b) What is the difference between the number of apples and the number of kiwis sold?

(c) What percentage of the fruits sold were oranges?

(d) He earned $33.75 from selling all the oranges. How much did he earn from selling each orange?

9 Angles

The following figures are not drawn to scale.

Worked Example 1

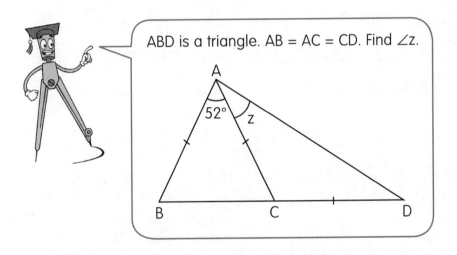

ABD is a triangle. AB = AC = CD. Find ∠z.

$\angle ABC = \angle ACB$ (base angles of isosceles triangle)

     $= (180° - 52°) \div 2$

     $= 64°$

$\angle ACD = 180° - 64°$ (angles on a straight line)

     $= 116°$

$\angle z = \angle CDA$ (base angles of isosceles triangle)

     $= (180° - 116°) \div 2$

     $= \mathbf{32°}$

Worked Example 2

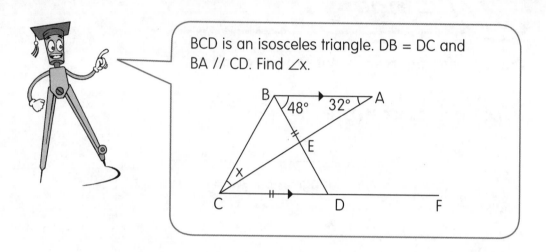

BCD is an isosceles triangle. DB = DC and BA // CD. Find ∠x.

∠AEB = 180° − 48° − 32°　　　(sum of angles in triangle)
　　　= 100°

∠CEB = 180° − 100°　　　　　(supplementary angles)
　　　= 80°

∠FDE = 180° − 48°　　　　　(pair of angles between 2 parallel
　　　= 132°　　　　　　　　　sides = 180°)

∠BDC = 180° − 132°　　　　　(supplementary angles)
　　　= 48°

∠DBC = (180° − 48°) ÷ 2　　　(base angles of isosceles triangle)
　　　= 66°

∠x = 180° − ∠DBC − ∠CEB　　(sum of angles in triangle)
　　= 180° − 66° − 80°
　　= **34°**

Practice Questions

**The following figures are not drawn to scale.
Answer all questions.**

1. PQRS is a rectangle, QY = PY, and RX = SZ. Find ∠XYZ.

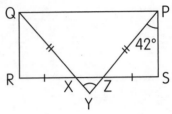

2. ABD is an equilateral triangle. BCD is an isosceles triangle. Find ∠x.

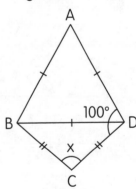

3. LMNO is a square. Find ∠p.

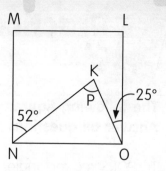

4. PQRS is a square and PQX is a straight line. Find ∠SQY.

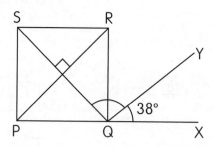

5. ABC and ADE are similar isosceles triangles. EAB, DYC, and XYZ are straight lines. Find ∠ADY.

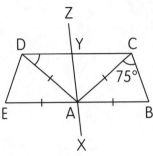

6. Noah is facing west. He first makes a quarter turn in the counterclockwise direction. Next, he turns clockwise through 215°.
   (a) What is the total angle he has turned?
   (b) What angle must he turn in the clockwise direction in order to face west again?

7. ABC is an equilateral triangle. If AD = DB = BF = FE and BD // FE, find ∠AEG.

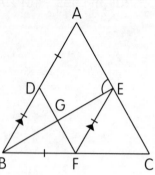

8. PQRS is a parallelogram, ABC is an isosceles triangle, and QR // AB. Find ∠y.

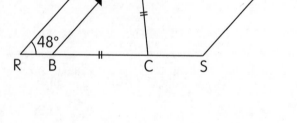

9. If the minute hand of a clock turns 240°, what angle does the hour hand of the clock turn?

10. The figure below is made up of four equilateral triangles. It has two lines of symmetry as shown. Find ∠TOU.

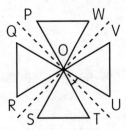

Challenging Problems

The following figures are not drawn to scale.

Worked Example 1

ABC is a triangle. AB = AC and $\angle BAC = 50°$. If $\angle DBC = \angle DCA$, find $\angle BDC$.

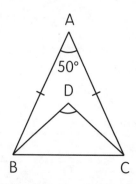

$\angle BCA = \angle CBA$ (base angles of isosceles triangle)

    $= (180° - 50°) \div 2$

    $= 65°$

$\angle DBC + \angle BCD = \angle BCA$

            $= 65°$

$\angle BDC = 180° - 65°$ (sum of angles in triangle)

      $= \mathbf{115°}$

The following figures are not drawn to scale.
Answer all questions.

1. PQRS is a square. PQA and QRB are equilateral triangles. Find ∠ABQ.

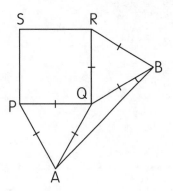

2. PQRS is a trapezoid. POS, SOR, ROQ, and QOP are isosceles triangles.

   OP = OQ = OR = OS and PS // QR. Given that ∠POS = $\frac{1}{2}$∠QOR, find ∠RQO.

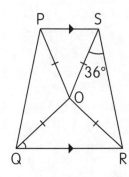

3. PQRS is a parallelogram. Find ∠y.

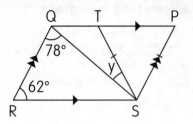

4. PQR is an isosceles triangle. QP = PR and QP // RT. Find ∠x.

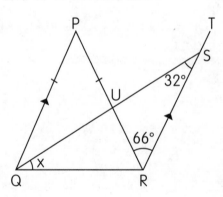

5. PQRS is a rectangle. If UW // TR and UT // VQ, find ∠x.

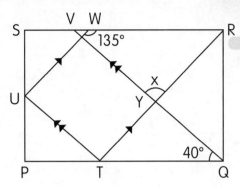

6. ABCD is a square. CDE is an equilateral triangle. Find ∠AEB.

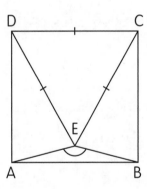

7. PQR is a triangle and PS = QS = RS. If ∠SRP = x°, find ∠QPR.

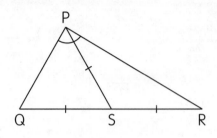

8. ABCD is a quadrilateral. DC = DB = DA. Find ∠x, ∠y, and ∠z.

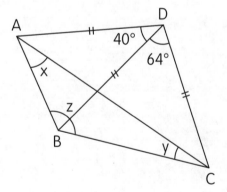

9. In the figure below, PQ and RS are straight lines that intersect at point O. XO ⊥ PQ and YO ⊥ RS. Find ∠a.

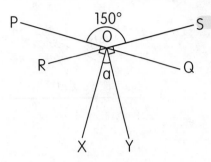

10. Find the unknown angles in the following figures.

(a)

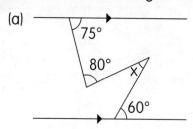

75°
80°
x
60°

(b)

83°
x
75°
65°
55°

10 Mixed Problems 1

Worked Example 1

When Jose stands on a chair of height 30 cm and Allison stands on a stool, Jose is 65 cm taller than Allison. When both of them stand on the floor, Jose is 70 cm taller than Allison. What is the height of the stool?

When both stand on the floor

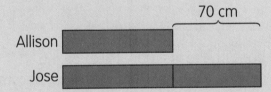

When Jose stands on the chair and Allison stands on the stool

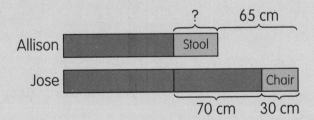

From the model, the height of the stool = 70 cm + 30 cm − 65 cm
= 35 cm

The height of the stool is **35 cm**.

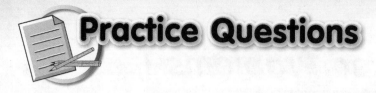

Practice Questions

Answer all questions.

1. The bells of a clock tower take 5 s to strike 6 times at six o'clock. How long will it take for the bells to strike 12 times at midnight?

2. Sierra put 1 coin into her piggy bank on the first day, 1 coin on the second day, 2 coins on the third day and so on. Her piggy bank became full on the tenth day. On which day was the piggy bank half full?

3. In a company, each employee works an equal whole number of hours a day. The total number of hours worked by all the employees each day is 161 h. If each employee works less than 10 h a day, how many employees are there?

4. Esther has $\frac{5}{8}$ as many cards as Andy. If Esther gives $\frac{3}{10}$ of her cards to Andy, what fraction of Andy's cards are Esther's cards?

5. A pail containing 60 plastic balls weigh 96 kg. A similar pail containing 80 plastic balls weigh 126 kg. Find the weight of the empty pail.

6. Bag F is 1.8 kg heavier than Bag G. Bags F, G, and H weigh 58.7 kg in all. If Bag H weighs 23.3 kg, how much does Bag F weigh?

7. Henry saves 50¢ every day. Kaylee saves 20¢ more than Henry every day. Kaylee starts saving up 8 days after Henry. If she has saved $10 more than Henry now, how much is her current savings?

8. Rachel had $560 and her sister had $120. After their father gave each of them an equal amount of money, Rachel had three times as much money as her sister. How much did their father give each of them?

9. Mrs. Makayla had 400 pumpkins and tomatoes. She sold $\frac{3}{4}$ of the pumpkins and $\frac{2}{3}$ of the tomatoes. She then had 120 pumpkins and tomatoes left. What fraction of the fruits were tomatoes at first?

10. Mr. Carey is 42 years old and his son is 10 years old. In how many years' time will he be 3 times as old as his son?

Challenging Problems

Worked Example 1

Two rulers and three pens cost $13. Four rulers and five pens cost $23.
What is the total cost of three rulers and four pens?

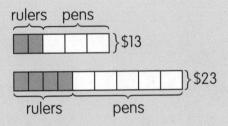

Cost of 1 pen = 2 × $13 − $23
$\qquad\quad$ = $26 − $23
$\qquad\quad$ = $3
Cost of 3 pens = 3 × $3
$\qquad\qquad$ = $9

Cost of 2 rulers = $13 − $9
$\qquad\qquad\quad$ = $4
Cost of 1 ruler = $4 ÷ 2
$\qquad\qquad$ = $2

Cost of 3 rulers + 4 pens = 3 × $2 + 4 × $3
$\qquad\qquad\qquad\qquad$ = $6 + $12
$\qquad\qquad\qquad\qquad$ = $18

The total cost of three rulers and four pens is **$18**.

Answer all questions.

1. The sum of two decimals is 20.89. The difference between these two decimals is 5.19. What is the product of the two decimals?

2. A box containing 30 pins weigh 80 g. A similar box containing 45 pins weigh 110 g. How much does the empty box weigh? How much does each pin weigh?

3. In a school cafeteria, a cup of tea costs 50¢ and a piece of cake costs 40¢. Some students went to the cafeteria and each of them bought the same number of cups of tea and the same number of pieces of cake. The total bill was $9.80.
   (a) How many students were there?
   (b) How many cups of tea and pieces of cake did each student have?

4. 429 students from some schools took part in last year's Math Olympiad competition. Each school sent in the same number of students. If each school sent in more than 20 students, how many schools took part in the competition?

5. The pages of a self-help book are numbered from 1 to 500. How many page numbers contain the digit five and are also divisible by five?

6. At a committee meeting, there were 4 times as many boys as girls. After 60 boys and 12 girls left halfway through the meeting, there were twice as many boys as girls. How many boys were there at first?

7. Oliver lost 10 tokens to Jill in a game. He then had 4 times as many tokens as her. If he had lost 44 tokens to her, he would have $1\frac{1}{2}$ times as many tokens as her. How many tokens did Oliver have at first?

8. Jennifer has 260 fewer guavas than kiwis at her fruits stall. $\frac{2}{3}$ of the number of guavas is equal to $\frac{1}{4}$ of the number of kiwis. All the guavas were sold to 6 customers. If each customer bought the same number of guavas, how many guavas did each customer buy?

9. The figure below shows a circle of diameter 6 cm, two semicircles of diameter 4 cm, and two semicircles of diameter 2 cm. Find the ratio of the area of region P to the area of region Q to the area of region R.

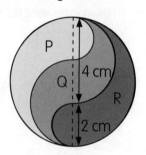

10. The figure below is made up of one big circle and four small circles of equal sizes. The diameter of each small circle is 6 cm. Express the total area of the four small circles as a fraction of the area of the shaded part.

11 Mixed Problems 2

Worked Example 1

The highest possible score Dave can obtain for each of his four tests is 100 points. His mean score was 82 points. What was the lowest possible score that he could have obtained on one test?

Total score for 4 tests = 4 × 82
$$= 328$$

Lowest possible score on one test = 328 − 3 × 100
$$= 28$$

The lowest possible score that he could have obtained on one test was **28** points.

Practice Questions

Answer all questions.

1. Town V and Town W are 200 mi apart. A train traveling at 75 mph leaves Town W for Town V. Another train traveling at 60 mph leaves Town V for Town W. If the trains travel at the same speed throughout the journey, how far apart are the trains one hour before they pass each other?

2. A van travels east at a speed of 50 km/h. A car travels west at a speed of 60 km/h. If both vehicles start traveling at the same time and from the same place, how long will it take them to be 220 km apart?

3. ABCD and PQRS are squares. P, Q, R, and S are midpoints of DA, AB, CB, and DC respectively. What fraction of the figure is shaded?

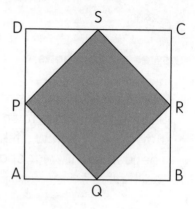

4. ABCD is a rhombus. Find ∠ADC.

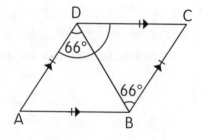

5. ABCD is a parallelogram. Find ∠x.

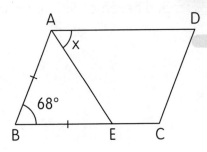

6. A train is traveling along a railway track. 16 poles can be found along the track. They are placed at an equal distance from one another. The train takes 6 min to travel from the 1st pole to the 10th pole. How long will it take to reach the 16th pole?

7. The mean of seven numbers is 8. An eighth number is added and the mean becomes 9. What is the eighth number?

8. Kimberly scored the following points in three test papers.

Paper	English	Math	Science
Points scored	50	80	100
Maximum points	80	100	120

Which test paper did Kimberly do best in?

9. PQRS is a parallelogram. Find ∠SQR.

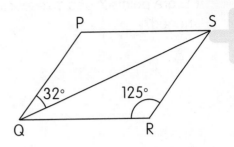

10. DEFG is a trapezoid. DG // EF. Find ∠DEF and ∠GFE.

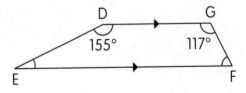

11. The figure below shows a rectangle ABCD. The midpoints of AB and CD are points X and Y respectively. What fraction of the rectangle is shaded?

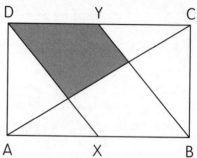

12. ABC is an equilateral triangle. XYZ is an isosceles triangle. XZ // BC. Find ∠YZC.

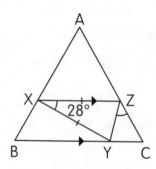

Challenging Problems

Worked Example 1

Machine A can produce 12,000 toys in 2 h. Machine B can produce 12,000 toys in 3 h. If both machines are turned on and producing toys at a constant rate, how long will it take both machines to produce 24,000 toys?

In 1 h, Machine A can produce $12{,}000 \div 2 = 6000$ toys.

In 1 h, Machine B can produce $12{,}000 \div 3 = 4000$ toys.

In 1 h, both machines can produce $6000 + 4000 = 10{,}000$ toys.

Time needed to make 24,000 toys $= 24{,}000 \div 10{,}000$

$$= 2\frac{2}{5}\ h$$

It will take both machines $2\frac{2}{5}$ **h** to produce 24,000 toys.

Answer all questions.

1. The figure below is made up of two right triangles. Find the sum of ∠QPS and ∠QRS.

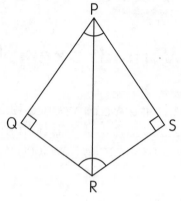

2. In the figure below, AC and BD are straight lines. They intersect at right angles at point E. If AE = 7.5 cm, BE = 6 cm, CE = 5 cm, and DE = 4 cm, find the value of $\dfrac{\text{area of triangle ADE}}{\text{area of triangle BCE}}$.

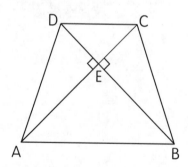

3. How many times each day do the hour and minute hands of an analog clock form a right angle?

4. Autumn and Diego jogged from Neighborhood A to Neighborhood B at constant speeds. Autumn took 3 h to complete the whole journey. Diego took 2 h to jog $\frac{3}{4}$ of the journey. Find the ratio of Autumn's speed to Diego's.

5. At a summer camp, 40 kg of cereal are provided for 30 campers to consume for 14 days.
   (a) If 5 more campers join the camp, how many days will the same quantity of cereal last?
   (b) If an additional 20 kg of cereal are donated and 10 more campers join the camp, how many days longer will the cereal last for the campers?

6. Van A and Van B traveled from Town X to Town Y at 100 km/h and 120 km/h respectively. Van A left Town X one hour before Van B. Both vans arrived in Town Y at the same time. Find the distance between the two towns.

7. Suzanne is thinking of 5 different whole numbers.
    The mean of the numbers is 30.
    The median is 35.
    The range is 20.
    The greatest number is 39.
    What is the greatest possible value for the second number?

8. In the figure below, $\frac{3}{5}$ of the small circle and $\frac{1}{6}$ of the big circle is shaded. What fraction of the figure is shaded?

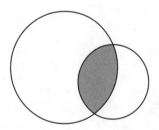

For the shaded area, we look for a common ratio for both circles.

9. The figure below shows a circle in a rectangle. The length and width of the rectangle is 30 cm and 20 cm respectively. What is the area of the shaded part? (Take π = 3.14)

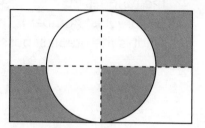

10. In the figure below, PQ = 14 cm. What is the total area of the shaded parts? (Take $\pi = \frac{22}{7}$)

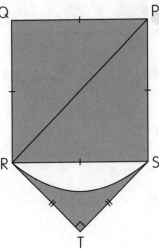

12 Mixed Problems 3

Worked Example 1

What is the value of each expression when $p = -3$ and $q = -1$?
(a) $q - 2p + 5$
(b) $q - 2(p + 5)$

(a) $q - 2p + 5 = (-1) - 2(-3) + 5$
$= (-1) + 6 + 5$
$= (-1) + 11$
$= \mathbf{10}$

(b) $q - 2(p + 5) = (-1) - 2[(-3) + 5]$
$= (-1) - 2(2)$
$= (-1) - 4$
$= \mathbf{-5}$

Worked Example 2

Catherine has three dimes and five quarters in her purse. She randomly picks a coin from her purse. Find the probability that the coin is
(a) a dime.
(b) a quarter.

Total number of coins in her purse = 3 + 5
                                    = 8

(a) There are three dimes in her purse.

The probability that the coin is a dime is $\frac{3}{8}$.

(b) There are five quarters in her purse.

The probability that the coin is a quarter is $\frac{5}{8}$.

Practice Questions

Answer all questions.

1. A scuba diver dives to 83 ft. below sea level, then swims back up by 47 ft. What is the diver's final position below the sea level?

2. At 11:00 p.m., the temperature in New York was −3°C. Within two hours, the temperature increased by 4°C. What was the temperature at 1:00 a.m.?

3. An elevator goes up 5 floors from the main lobby, then goes up another 3 more floors, before going down 10 floors. Which floor is it at now?

4. A plane rose at a rate of 2250 ft. per minute for 8 min after taking off from Honolulu International Airport. The plane then descended at a rate of 1750 ft. per minute for 3 min. What was its final vertical height above sea level?

5. The graph shows the line $y = 1 - 2x$. Use the graph to solve each equation.
   (a) $1 - 2x = 3$
   (b) $1 - 2x = -3$
   (c) $1 - 2x = 0$

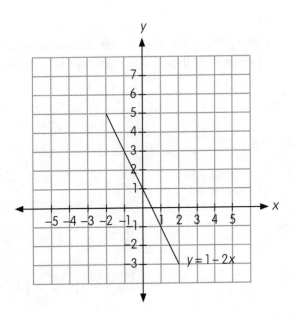

6. Complete the table and graph $y = 2 - x$.

x				1	
y				1	

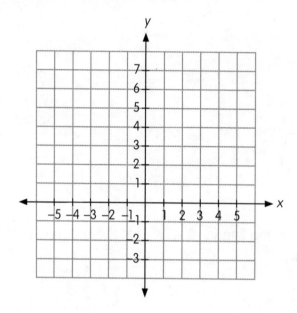

7. The probability that it will rain on any day in July is 0.3. Find the probability that it will rain on two consecutive days in July.

8. Evan tosses a coin three times in a row. Find the probability that he gets heads three times.

9. A box contains 1 red card, 3 blue cards, and 4 green cards. A card is randomly drawn from the box. Find the probability that it is
    (a) a red card.
    (b) a green card.
    (c) a red or green card.

10. Peter rolls a regular six-sided die. Find the probability that the die does not show a multiple of 3.

Challenging Problems

Worked Example 1

Sara wants to make a label consisting of five characters.
Three different label makers are available.

Label Maker	Requirement
1	Labels have 3 letters followed by 2 digits. Letters and digits can be repeated.
2	Labels have 2 letters followed by 3 digits. Letters and digits can be repeated.
3	Labels have 5 digits. Digits can be repeated.

Which label maker produces the greatest number of different labels?
Explain your answer.

There are 26 letters (A, B, ..., Z) and 10 digits (0, 1, 2, 3, ..., 9)
to choose from.

For Label Maker 1, since both letters and digits can be repeated, the
number of choices is $26 \times 26 \times 26 \times 10 \times 10$.

For Label Maker 2, since both letters and digits can be repeated, the
number of choices is $26 \times 26 \times 10 \times 10 \times 10$.

For Label Maker 3, since digits can be repeated, the number of
choices is $10 \times 10 \times 10 \times 10 \times 10$.

From the factors of each label maker, **Label Maker 1** produces the
greatest number of different labels.

Answer all questions.

1. Fill in the blanks with *greater, smaller, colder,* or *warmer.*

   (a) 15 is _____ than 12.

       15°C is _____ than 12°C.

   (b) 0 is _____ than 2.

       0°C is _____ than 2°C.

   (c) −6°C is _____ than 0°C.

       −6 is _____ than 0.

   (d) −9°C is _____ than −6°C.

       −9 is _____ than −6.

   (e) 0°C is _____ than −3°C.

       0 is _____ than −3.

   (f) −12°C is _____ than −15°C.

       −12 is _____ than −15.

2. Solve these equations.

   (a) $\frac{3}{5}y = -6$ (b) $q - 3 = -5$

   (c) $2 - p = 5$ (d) $3 - x = -5$

3. Aiden has 4 pairs of socks and 2 pairs of shoes. The colors of his socks are black, white, brown, and grey. The colors of his shoes are black and red. If Aiden wants to match a pair of socks to a pair of shoes, what is the probability of matching
   (a) the black pair of shoes to the white or brown pair of socks?
   (b) the black and red pair of shoes to the black or grey pair of socks?

4. A total of 15 cards with the letters A, C, D, E, G, I, J, L, M, N, O, S, T, U, and Y are put into a box. Two cards are drawn randomly. The first card drawn is not replaced. Find the probability that both cards drawn show consonants.

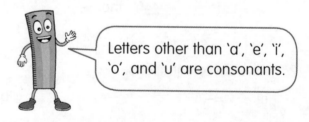

Letters other than 'a', 'e', 'i', 'o', and 'u' are consonants.

5. Landon rolls a regular six-sided die twice. Find the probability that he gets a 6 the first time and an odd number the second time.

6. The names of 6 students are written on small pieces of paper and placed in a hat.

| Adam | Bob | Cathy | Dawn | Esther | Fabian |

Mrs. Paula draws two names randomly.
(a) Find the probability that the first name drawn is a boy's name.
(b) Find the probability that the second name drawn is a boy's name, given that the first name drawn is Dawn.
(c) Find the probability that both names drawn are boys' names.

7. Julia rolls two regular six-sided dice. What is the probability that the sum of the scores on the dice is a multiple of 5?

8. There are some U.S., Singapore, and China stamps in an envelope. The probability of picking a U.S. stamp is $\frac{1}{3}$. The probability of picking a Singapore stamp is $\frac{2}{9}$. There are 12 China stamps. How many stamps are there in the envelope?

9. There are some pyramids, rectangular prisms, and cylinders in a box. Use the following clues to figure out the number of blocks in the box.

Clues:
- The probability of picking a pyramid is $\frac{1}{2}$.
- The probability of picking a rectangular prism is $\frac{1}{3}$.
- There are 9 cylinders.

(a) How many blocks are in the box?
(b) How many pyramids are in the box?
(c) How many rectangular prisms are in the box?

10. A coin has both a head and a tail. A spinner has 5 equal parts numbered 1 to 5.
   (a) How many possible outcomes are there when the coin is tossed and the spinner is spun?
   (b) What is the theoretical probability of getting
      (i)   a tail and a 5?
      (ii) a head and a 0?
      (iii) a tail and an odd number?
      (iv) a head and an even number?

Answers

1 Algebra

Practice Questions (pp. 3–7)

1. (a) $x + 3$ (b) $x - 2$
   (c) $4x$ (d) $\frac{1}{5}x$ or $\frac{x}{5}$

2. $\dfrac{10}{p}$

3. $7a$ days

4. $\dfrac{x}{y}$ apples

5. (a) $\dfrac{p}{60}$ h   (b) $\dfrac{q}{7}$ weeks

6. (a) $2(a + b)$ cm   (b) ab cm^2

7. $(u - v + w)$ coins

8. $x = \dfrac{25}{8}$
   $= 3\dfrac{1}{8}$

9. p miles $\longrightarrow$ q gal
   1 mile $\longrightarrow \dfrac{q}{7}$ gal
   r miles $\longrightarrow \dfrac{q}{p} \times r = \dfrac{qr}{p}$ gal

10. $m = (4a + 3) - (2a + 1)$
    $= (2a + 2)$ in.
    $n = (3b + 1) - b$
    $= (2b + 1)$ in.

11. $\dfrac{9 + 8 + 7}{1 \times 2 \times 3} = 4$

12. $a^\circ + b^\circ + 36^\circ = 180^\circ$
    $a^\circ + b^\circ = 180^\circ - 36^\circ$
    $= 144^\circ$
    $a^\circ + 3a^\circ = 144^\circ$
    $4a^\circ = 144^\circ$
    $a = 144 \div 4$
    $= 36$
    $b = 3a$
    $= 3 \times 36$
    $= 108$

Challenging Problems (pp. 11–14)

1. **Method 1**

         10   2

3 units $\longrightarrow$ $10 + 2 = 12$
1 unit $\longrightarrow$ $12 \div 3 = 4$
The value of n is 4.

Method 2

$5n - 2 = 2n + 10$
$5n - 2 + 2 = 2n + 10 + 2$
$5n = 2n + 12$
$5n - 2n = 12$
$3n = 12$
$n = 12 \div 3$
$= 4$

2. $52x - 13y = 65$
   $13 \times (4x - y) = 65$
   $4x - y = 65 \div 13$
   $= 5$
   $28x - 7y = 7 \times (4x - y)$
   $= 7 \times 5$
   $= 35$

3. 136 cm$^2 = 100$ cm$^2 + 36$ cm^2
   $= 10$ cm $\times$ 10 cm $+$ 6 cm $\times$ 6 cm
   $y = 10$ cm
   $x = 6$ cm
   $(x + y) = 6$ cm $+$ 10 cm
   $= 16$ cm

4. (a)

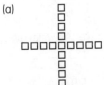

Figure 5

Note that there is 1 □ in the middle, and
4 arms, each of which has 1 □ less than
the number given to each figure.

Figure	1	2	3	4	5
Number of cubes needed	$4 \times (1 - 1) + 1$ $= 1$	$4 \times (2 - 1) + 1$ $= 5$	$4 \times (3 - 1) + 1$ $= 9$	$4 \times (4 - 1) + 1$ $= 13$	$4 \times (5 - 1) + 1$ $= 17$
Figure	...	(b) 7	...	(b) 12	(c) n
Number of cubes needed	...	$4 \times (7 - 1) + 1$ $= \mathbf{25}$	...	$4 \times (12 - 1) + 1$ $= \mathbf{45}$	$4 \times (n - 1) + 1$ $= \mathbf{4n - 3}$

5. (a)

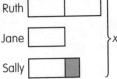

        25

4 units $\longrightarrow$ $x - 25$
1 unit $\longrightarrow$ $\left(\dfrac{x - 25}{4}\right)$

Jane took $\left(\dfrac{x - 25}{4} + 25\right)$ candies.

(b) if x = 265,

Jane took $\frac{265 - 25}{4} = \frac{240}{4}$

= 60 candies

Ruth took 2 × 60 = 120 candies.

Sally took 60 + 25 = 85 candies

6. (a) 2 × $0.80 + 2 × $1.20 = $1.60 + $2.40

= $4.00

(b) 2 × $0.90 + $0.80 + 2 × $1.30 + $1.20

= $1.80 + $0.80 + $2.60 + $1.20

= $6.40

(c) (80m + 90n)¢ or $(0.8m + 0.9n)

(d) (120p + 130q)¢ or $(1.2p + 1.3q)

(e) (80a + 90b + 120c + 130d)¢ or
$(0.8a + 0.9b + 1.2c + 1.3d)

7.

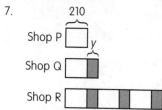

(a) From the model, Shop R has
= 3y + 2 × 210 = (3y + 420) more
television sets than Shop P.

(b) 4y = 4 × 110

= 440

5 × 210 + 440 = 1490

The three shops have 1490 television
sets in all.

8. 20(w − 1) ft.

9. Length of first string = x cm

Length of second string = (x − 2) cm

Length of third string = (x − 2) cm

x + (30 − 1)(x − 2) = x + 29(x − 2) cm

The total length of the strings is
x + 29(x − 2) cm.

10. Cost of 1 apple = p¢

Cost of 1 orange = (p + q)¢

Cost of 2 apples = 2p¢

Cost of 3 oranges = 3 × (p + q)¢

= (3p + 3q)¢

2p¢ + 3p¢ + 3q¢ = (5p + 3q)¢

The total cost of 2 apples and 3 oranges is
(5p + 3q)¢.

2 Fractions

Practice Questions (pp. 16–21)

1.

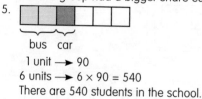

3 units → 18

1 unit → 18 ÷ 3 = 6

5 units → 5 × 6 = 30

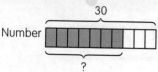

10 units → 30

1 unit → 30 ÷ 10 = 3

7 units → 7 × 3 = 21

$\frac{7}{10}$ of the number is 21.

2. 324 people

3. $\frac{2}{5}$ ft. + $\frac{3}{4}$ ft. = $\frac{8}{20}$ ft. + $\frac{15}{20}$ ft.

$= \frac{23}{20}$ ft.

$= 1\frac{3}{20}$ ft.

String Q is $1\frac{3}{20}$ ft. long.

$\frac{23}{20}$ ft. − $\frac{7}{10}$ ft. = $\frac{23}{20}$ ft. − $\frac{14}{20}$ ft.

$= \frac{9}{20}$ ft.

String R is $\frac{9}{20}$ ft. long.

$\frac{2}{5}$ ft. + $\frac{23}{20}$ ft. + $\frac{9}{20}$ ft. = $\frac{8}{20}$ ft. + $\frac{23}{20}$ ft. + $\frac{9}{20}$ ft.

$= \frac{40}{20}$ ft.

= 2 ft.

The total length of strings P, Q, and R is 2 ft.

4. Each share in Kelvin's group = $3\frac{1}{5} \div 8$

$= \frac{16}{5} \times \frac{1}{8}$

$= \frac{2}{5}$

$= \frac{16}{40}$

Each share in Jane's group = $2\frac{5}{8} \div 7$

$= \frac{21}{8} \times \frac{1}{7}$

$= \frac{3}{8}$

$= \frac{15}{40}$

Since $\frac{16}{40}$ is greater than $\frac{15}{40}$, $\frac{2}{5}$ is greater
than $\frac{3}{8}$.

Kelvin's group had a bigger share each.

5.

bus car

1 unit → 90

6 units → 6 × 90 = 540

There are 540 students in the school.

6. 50 coins

7. 200 cards

8. 128 stamps

9.
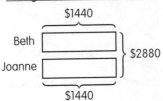

Daisy

135

Henry

5 units ⟶ 135
1 unit ⟶ 135 ÷ 5 = 27
11 units ⟶ 11 × 27 = 297
They have 297 stickers in all.

10. Both girls had the same amount of money

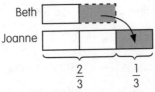

$1440

Beth

Joanne

$2880

$1440

Joanne gave $\frac{1}{3}$ of the total amount she had to Beth

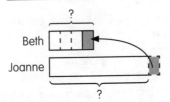

Beth

Joanne

$\frac{2}{3}$ $\frac{1}{3}$

2 units ⟶ $1440
1 unit ⟶ $1440 ÷ 2 = $720

Beth gave $\frac{1}{4}$ of her money to Joanne

?

Beth

Joanne

?

(a) 3 units ⟶ $720
1 unit ⟶ $720 ÷ 3 = $240
4 units ⟶ 4 × $240 = $960
Beth had $960 at first.
(b) $2880 − $960 = $1920
Joanne had $1920 at first.

11. Small ball bearing

Big ball bearing

If 2 units represent 1 small ball bearing, then 20 units represent 10 small ball bearings.
Possible combinations of ball bearings that represent 20 units are:

Big ball bearing	Small ball bearing	Total
6	1	6 × 3 + 1 × 2 = 20
4	4	4 × 3 + 4 × 2 = 20
2	7	2 × 3 + 7 × 2 = 20

6 big and 1 small ball bearings or 4 big and 4 small ball bearings or 2 big and 7 small ball bearings will be needed to balance 10 small ball bearings.

12. **Method 1**

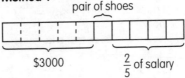

pair of shoes

$3000 $\frac{2}{5}$ of salary

5 units ⟶ $3000
1 unit ⟶ $3000 ÷ 5 = $600
10 units ⟶ 10 × $600 = $6000
His salary was $6000.

Method 2

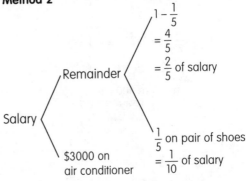

$$1 - \frac{1}{5} = \frac{4}{5} = \frac{2}{5} \text{ of salary}$$

Remainder

$\frac{1}{5}$ on pair of shoes = $\frac{1}{10}$ of salary

Salary

$3000 on air conditioner

Remainder = $\frac{2}{5} ÷ \frac{4}{5}$
= $\frac{2}{5} × \frac{5}{4}$
= $\frac{1}{2}$

Fraction representing $3000 = 1 − $\frac{1}{2}$
= $\frac{1}{2}$

Total salary = 2 × $3000
= $6000
His salary was $6000.

Challenging Problems (pp. 23–27)

1. 64 stickers

2.
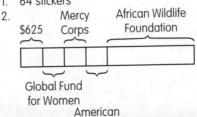

$625   Mercy Corps   African Wildlife Foundation

Global Fund for Women

American Red Cross

1 unit ⟶ $625
4 units ⟶ 4 × $625 = $2500
So he must have 2 × $2500 = $5000 at first.
3. 20th day: completely covered
19th day: $\frac{1}{2}$ covered

18th day: $\frac{1}{4}$ covered
$\frac{1}{4}$ of the surface of the pond was covered on the 18th day.

4. (a) In 5 days, Cherie reads $\frac{1}{5}$ of the book.

In 1 day, she reads $\frac{1}{5} \div 5 = \frac{1}{25}$ of the book.
In 8 days, she reads $8 \times \frac{1}{25} = \frac{8}{25}$ of the book.
Fraction of the book that she reads
$= \frac{1}{5} + \frac{8}{25}$
$= \frac{13}{25}$
$1 - \frac{13}{25} = \frac{12}{25}$
$\frac{12}{25}$ of the book is not read.

(b) $\frac{12}{25}$ ⟶ 192

$\frac{1}{25}$ ⟶ 192 ÷ 12 = 16

$\frac{25}{25}$ ⟶ 25 × 16 = 400

There are 400 pages in the book.

5.
Melons

260

Pineapples

8 − 3 = 5 units
5 units ⟶ 260
1 unit ⟶ 260 ÷ 5 = 52
3 units ⟶ 3 × 52 = 156
6 customers bought 156 melons.
156 ÷ 6 = 26
Each customer bought 26 melons.

6.
spent

Mrs. Jones

$720

Claire

$150

19 units ⟶ $720 − $150 = $570
1 unit ⟶ $570 ÷ 19 = $30
5 units ⟶ 5 × $30 = $150
$150 + $150 = $300
Claire had $300 at first.

7. Let the number of red balls be $4R$ and the number of green balls be $5G$.
$R + 2G = 21$ (given)
$3R + 4G = 47$ (given)

$2R + 2G = 47 - 21$
$\qquad = 26$
$R = 26 - 21$
$\quad = 5$
$4R = 4 \times 5$
$\quad\;\; = 20$ (red balls)
$2G = 21 - 5$
$\quad\;\; = 16$
$G = 16 \div 2$
$\quad = 8$
$5G = 5 \times 8$
$\quad\;\; = 40$ (green balls)
There are 20 red balls and 40 green balls.

8. **Method 1**
$\frac{4}{7}$ of the money ⟶ $420

$\frac{1}{7}$ of the money ⟶ $420 ÷ 4 = $105

$\frac{7}{7}$ of the money ⟶ $7 × $105 = $735

$\frac{1}{8}$ of her savings ⟶ $735

$\frac{8}{8}$ of her savings ⟶ 8 × $735 = $5880

She had $5880 in her bank account at first.
Method 2
Let the amount of money in her bank account be 8 × 7 = 56 units.

She withdrew $\frac{1}{8}$ × 56 = 7 units.

Then she used $\frac{4}{7}$ × 7 = 4 units to buy the coffee table.
4 units ⟶ $420
1 unit ⟶ $420 ÷ 4 = $105
56 units ⟶ 56 × $105 = $5880
She had $5880 in her bank account at first.

9.
Mangoes   Grapefruits

400

120

3 × 120 = 360

1 ⟶ 400 − 360 = 40

4 ⟶ 4 × 40 = 160

3 ⟶ 400 − 160 = 240

$\frac{240}{400} = \frac{3}{5}$

$\frac{3}{5}$ of the fruits were mangoes at first.

10. Method 1

Tables

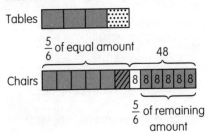

$\frac{5}{6}$ of equal amount   48

Chairs   8 8 8 8 8 8

$\frac{5}{6}$ of remaining amount

▦ + ▨ + 8 = 33

$\frac{3}{2}$ ▨ + ▨ = 33 − 8 = 25

$\frac{5}{2}$ ▨ = 25

▨ ⟶ $25 \times \frac{3}{5} = 10$

▦ ⟶ $\frac{3}{2} \times 10 = 15$

(a) $4 \times 15 = 60$

There were 60 tables at first.

(b) Number of tables sold = 3×15

     = 45

Number of chairs sold = $5 \times 10 + 40$

     = 90

Total number of chairs and tables sold

     = 45 + 90

     = 135

$\frac{90}{135} = \frac{2}{3}$

$\frac{2}{3}$ of the items sold were chairs.

Method 2

(a) Let the number of tables be x. Let the number of chairs be $(x + 48)$.

$\frac{1}{4}x + \frac{1}{6}(x + 48) = 33$

$\frac{1}{4}x + \frac{1}{6}x + 8 = 33$

$\frac{3x + 2x}{12} = 33 - 8$

       $= 25$

$5x = 25 \times 12$

   $= 300$

$x = 300 \div 5$

   $= 60$

There were 60 tables at first.

(b) Number of tables sold = $\frac{3}{4} \times 60$

     = 45

Number of chairs sold = $\frac{5}{6} \times (60 + 48)$

     $= \frac{5}{6} \times 108$

     $= 5 \times 18$

     $= 90$

$\frac{90}{135} = \frac{2}{3}$

$\frac{2}{3}$ of the items sold were chairs.

3 Percentage

Practice Questions (pp. 30–34)

1. **Method 1**

Since Bob's earnings is 50% more than Ruth's, Bob's earnings is 150% of Ruth's earnings.

Since 150% = 1.5, Bob earns $1\frac{1}{2}$ times as much as Ruth.

Method 2

Ruth

Bob

Bob's earnings is $\frac{3}{2} \times 100\% = 150\%$ of Ruth's

earnings, or $1\frac{1}{2}$ times as much as Ruth.

2. Chocolate cookies

Other types of cookies

$\frac{1}{5} \times 100\% = 20\%$

20% of the cookies are chocolate cookies.

3. From 5% to 7%, there is an increase of 2%.

$\frac{2}{5} \times 100\% = 40\%$

There is a 40% increase in the discount.

4. (a) $0.10\% = \frac{0.1}{100}$

      $= 0.001$

$0.001 \times \$10{,}000 = \$10$

An interest of \$10 is earned on a \$10,000 deposit after a month.

(b) $\frac{1}{8}\% \times \$20{,}000 = \frac{1}{8} \times \frac{1}{100} \times \$20{,}000$

            $= \$25$

An interest of \$25 is earned after a month.

5. $\frac{3 - 2}{2} \times 100\% = \frac{1}{2} \times 100\%$

            $= 50\%$

There is a 50% increase in the toll.

6. February allowance

100% ⟶ \$45

   1% ⟶ $\$45 \div 100 = \$0.45$

125% ⟶ $125 \times \$0.45 = \$56.25$

March allowance

100% ⟶ \$56.25

   1% ⟶ $\$56.25 \div 100 = \$0.5625$

75% ⟶ $75 \times \$0.5625 \approx \$42.1875$

$45 - $42.1875 = $2.8125

$\dfrac{2.8125}{45} \times 100\% = 6.25\%$

There is a 6.25% increase in her allowance in March as compared to her allowance in January.

7. 93% of the total number of bricks ordered must be at least 10,000 as 7% of the bricks may be broken on delivery.

93% ⟶ 10,000

$100\% \longrightarrow \dfrac{10,000}{93} \times 100 \approx 10,753$
$\approx 10,800$

He should order at least 10,800 bricks to finish building the house.

8. $\dfrac{60 + 100}{80 + 120} \times 100\% = 80\%$

Her overall score is 80%

9. Let the number be 100.
105% of 100 = 1.05 × 100
= 105
90% of 105 = 0.90 × 105
= 94.5
90% of 100 = 0.90 × 100
= 90
105% of 90 = 1.05 × 90
= 94.5

So an increase of 5% followed by a decrease of 10% is equivalent to a decrease of 10% followed by an increase of 5%.
Jay is correct.

10. **Method 1**
Boys: 75%
Girls: 25%

Number of boys = $\dfrac{75}{100} \times 140$
= 105

Number of girls = $\dfrac{25}{100} \times 140$
= 35

There are 105 − 35 = 70 more boys than girls.

$\dfrac{70}{35} \times 100\% = 200\%$

There are 200% more boys than girls.

Method 2

$\dfrac{75 - 25}{25} \times 100\% = \dfrac{50}{25} \times 100\%$
= 200%

There are 200% more boys than girls.

11.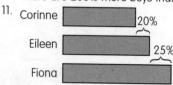

Corinne — 20%
Eileen — 25%
Fiona

Let the amount of money Eileen has be 100 units.
Corinne has 80% × 100 = 80 units.
Fiona has 125% × 100 = 125 units.

$\dfrac{80}{125} \times 100\% = 64\%$

The amount of money Corinne has is 64% of the amount of money Fiona has.

Challenging Problems (pp. 36–40)

1. Let the company's sales at the start of 2007 be 100 units.
In 2007, its sales increased to
110% × 100 = 110 units.
In 2008, its sales further increased to
120% × 110 = 132 units.
In 2009, its sales decreased to
80% × 132 = 105.6 units.
In 2010, its sales further decreased to
90% × 105.6 = 95.04 units.
100% − 95.04% = 4.96%
There was a 4.96% decrease in the company's sales.

2. Fraction of students who passed the first time
$= 1 - \dfrac{2}{3}$
$= \dfrac{1}{3}$

Fraction of students who passed the retest
$= \dfrac{40}{100} \times \dfrac{2}{3}$
$= \dfrac{4}{15}$

Fraction of students who pass after the retest
$= \dfrac{1}{3} + \dfrac{4}{15}$
$= \dfrac{5}{15} + \dfrac{4}{15}$
$= \dfrac{9}{15}$
$= \dfrac{3}{5}$

$\dfrac{3}{5} \times 100\% = 60\%$

60% of the students passed the test.

3. 25%

4. 82%

5. $5\% = \dfrac{5}{100}$
$= \dfrac{1}{20}$

$25\% = \dfrac{5}{20}$

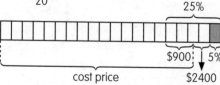

25%

$900   5%

cost price $2400

4 units → $900 + $2400 = $3300
1 unit → $3300 ÷ 4 = $825
19 units → 19 × $825 = $15,675
$15,675 − $2400 = $13,275
The cost price of the vintage watch set is $13,275.

6. Before

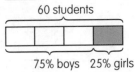

60 students

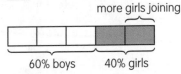

75% boys   25% girls

After

more girls joining

60% boys   40% girls

4 units → 60
1 unit → 60 ÷ 4 = 15
15 more girls join the class.

7. Out of 100 births, 3 are twins.
There are 103 babies in total, six of which are twins.
Percentage of newborn babies who are twins
$= \dfrac{6}{103} \times 100\%$
$\approx 6\%$
More than 3% of the newborn babies is made up of twins.

8. Solid weight of figs = 1% of 10 lbs
$= \dfrac{1}{100} \times 10$ lbs
$= \dfrac{1}{10}$ lb
Since the solid weight of the figs remains unchanged, after they were dried under the sun, 2% of the weight of the figs represent $\dfrac{1}{10}$ lb.
$2\% \rightarrow \dfrac{1}{10}$ lb = 0.1 lb
$1\% \rightarrow 0.1$ lb ÷ 2 = 0.05 lb
$100\% \rightarrow 100 \times 0.05$ lb = 5 lbs
The weight of the figs now is 5 lbs.

9. Number of watches at first $= \dfrac{60}{100} \times 1200$
$= 720$
Number of clocks at first = 1200 − 720
$= 480$
Percentage of watches now = 20%
Percentage of clocks now = 100% − 20%
$= 80\%$
80% → 480
20% → 480 ÷ 4 = 120 (number of watches left)
Number of watches sold = 720 − 120
$= 600$
600 watches were sold.

10. Let the original number of participants be 100 units.
60 units represent the number of men, and 40 units represent the number of women.
When 140 more participants joined in,
20% of 60 units $= \dfrac{20}{100} \times 60$
$= 12$ units
40% of 40 units $= \dfrac{40}{100} \times 40$
$= 16$ units
So, an extra 12 + 16 = 28 units were added.
28 units → 140
1 unit → 140 ÷ 28 = 5
The total number of participants in the end will be 100 + 28 = 128 units.
128 units → 128 × 5 = 640
There were 640 participants at the forum in the end.

4 Ratio

Practice Questions (pp. 44–48)

1. 2 : 3
2. 72 bookmarks
3. 5 : 17
4. 25 English books
5. Elizabeth: $24, Paul: $36
6. 48 dolls
7. 35 biscuits
8. 84 books
9. $75
10. 36 girls
11. (a) Before

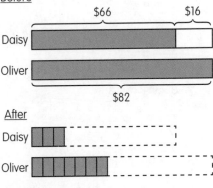

$66 $16

Daisy

Oliver

$82

After

Daisy

Oliver

4 units → $16
1 unit → $16 ÷ 4 = $4
3 + 7 = 10 units
10 units → 10 × $4 = $40
They have $40 left.

(b) $54

Challenging Problems (pp. 50–54)

1. 7 : 17
2. 30,000 pages
3. Total value of 18 nickels = 18 × 50¢
   = $9

   Number of nickels added = $\dfrac{10 - 9}{0.5}$
   = 2

Method 1
Before

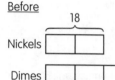

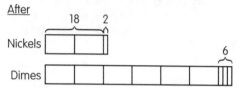

After

After

2 units → 18
1 unit → 18 ÷ 2 = 9
Number of dimes received = 3 units + 6
= 3 × 9 + 6
= 27 + 6
= 33
He received 33 dimes.

Method 2

Nickels : Dimes
Before   2x   :   3x
After   2x + 2 : 3x + y
2x = 18
x = 18 ÷ 2
= 9
Let y be the number of dimes he received.

$\dfrac{2x + 2}{3x + y} = \dfrac{1}{3}$

$\dfrac{2 \times 9 + 2}{3 \times 9 + y} = \dfrac{1}{3}$

$\dfrac{20}{27 + y} = \dfrac{1}{3}$

27 + y = 20 × 3
= 60
y = 60 – 27
= 33
He received 33 dimes.

4. Let the number of male voters be 17n and the number of female voters be 15n.

$\dfrac{17n - 90}{15n - 80} = \dfrac{8}{7}$

7 × (17n – 90) = 8 × (15n – 80)
119n – 630 = 120n – 640
n = 10

Number of people taking part in the election
= 17n + 15n
= 32n
= 32 × 10
= 320
320 people voted in the election.

5.
P	:	Q		R	:	P
= 2	:	5		= 4	:	7
= 14	:	35		= 8	:	14

P	:	Q	:	R
= 14	:	35	:	8

35 – 8 = 27 units
27 units → 8100
1 unit → 8100 ÷ 27 = 300
8 units → 8 × 300 = 2400
There are 2400 residents in Town R.

6.

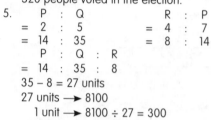

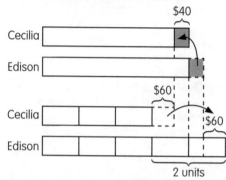

2 units → $60 + $40 + $40 + $60 = $200
1 unit → $200 ÷ 2 = $100
5 units – $60 = 5 × $100 – $60
= $500 – $60
= $440
Edison had $440 at first.

7.
P	:	Q	:	R
= 4	:	2	:	3
= 2	:	1		

Before

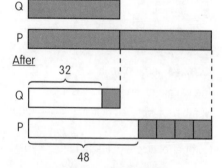

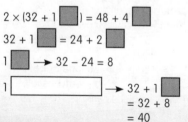

2 × (32 + 1 ⬛) = 48 + 4 ⬛
32 + 1 ⬛ = 24 + 2 ⬛
1 ⬛ → 32 – 24 = 8

1 ▭ → 32 + 1 ⬛
= 32 + 8
= 40

In the end, Basket R has

= 3 [⬚⬚⬚⬚⬚⬚⬚⬚] + 5 ▮

= 40 ÷ 2 × 3 + 5 × 8

= 60 + 40

= 100

There were 100 eggs in Basket R in the end.

8. Let the original length of Candle A be x and the original length of Candle B be y.

$$x - \frac{x}{9} = y - \frac{y}{6}$$

$$\frac{9x - 2x}{9} = \frac{6y - 2y}{6}$$

$$\frac{7x}{9} = \frac{4y}{6}$$

$$42x = 36y$$

$$\frac{x}{y} = \frac{36}{42}$$

$$= \frac{6}{7}$$

The ratio of the original length of Candle A to Candle B's is 6 : 7.

9. Before

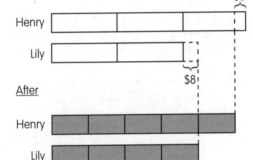

After

1 ▮ + $8 + $5 = 1 [⬚⬚⬚⬚]

1 ▮ + $13 = 1 [⬚⬚⬚]

3 [⬚⬚⬚] − $5 = 5 ▮

3 ▮ + $39 − $5 = 5 ▮

2 ▮ ⟶ $34

1 ▮ ⟶ $34 ÷ 2 = $17

4 ▮ ⟶ 4 × $17 = $68

$68 − $8 = $60

Lily had $60 at first.

10. Before

Quarters [⬚⬚⬚]

Dimes [⬚⬚⬚⬚⬚]

After

Quarters [⬚⬚] ⌐ ¬

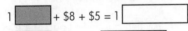

Dimes [⬚⬚⬚⬚⬚⬚⬚⬚⬚⬚⬚⬚]

---

2 units ⟶ 8 (quarters)

1 unit ⟶ 8 ÷ 2 = 4

12 units ⟶ 12 × 4 = 48 (dimes)

Total value of quarters = 8 × 25¢

= $2

Total value of dimes = 48 × 10¢

= $4.80

$2 + $4.80 = $6.80

Sam had $6.80.

5 Speed

Practice Questions (pp. 57–61)

1. In 1 h, Zachary and Dylan walk a total distance of 8 + 11 = 19 km.

$$4\frac{1}{2} \times 19 \text{ km} = 85\frac{1}{2} \text{ km}$$

They will be $85\frac{1}{2}$ km apart after $4\frac{1}{2}$ h.

2. 12 min

3. Car M

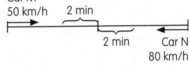

In 60 min, Car M travels 50 km.

In 2 min, Car M travels $\frac{50}{60} \times 2 = 1\frac{2}{3}$ km.

In 60 min, Car N travels 80 km.

In 2 min, Car M travels $\frac{80}{60} \times 2 = 2\frac{2}{3}$ km.

$1\frac{2}{3}$ km + $2\frac{2}{3}$ km = $4\frac{1}{3}$ km

The cars are $4\frac{1}{3}$ km apart 2 minutes before they pass each other.

4. Since one driver travels 15 mph faster than the other driver, this means that after every 1 h, one will be 15 m ahead of the other. The faster driver travels 100 − 75 = 25 mi more than the slower driver.

This 25 mi can be covered in $25 ÷ 15 = \frac{5}{3}$ h.

Thus, the whole journey takes $\frac{5}{3}$ h.

$100 \times \frac{3}{5} = 60$ mph

The speed of the car is 60 mph.

5. Since each bus travels at the same speed of 60 km/h, each will travel 30 ÷ 2 = 15 km before they meet each other.

60 km ⟶ 1 h = 60 min

15 km ⟶ 60 ÷ 4 = 15 min

It will take them 15 min to meet.

6. Ava will be 2 × 60 = 120 km ahead when Tyler starts off.

As Tyler is traveling at 90 − 60 = 30 km/h faster than Ava, he will close the gap in 120 ÷ 30 = 4 h.

Tyler will overtake Ava in 4 h.

7. 82.8 km/h

173

8. Time taken to travel 220 km = 220 ÷ 80

$$= 2\frac{3}{4} \text{ h}$$

45 min = $\frac{3}{4}$ h

$2\frac{3}{4}$ h + $\frac{3}{4}$ h = $3\frac{1}{2}$ h

It will take him $3\frac{1}{2}$ h to complete a 220-km journey.

9. Every 1 h, the car travels an extra distance of 80 − 70 = 10 km.

The car covers 10 km in 1 h.

The car covers 2 km in $\frac{1}{10}$ × 2 h

$$= \frac{1}{10} × 2 × 60 \text{ min}$$

$$= 12 \text{ min}$$

It will take the car 12 min to overtake the van.

10. If Paul drove at 50 mph instead of 40 mph, he would have covered an extra of 50 − 40 = 10 mi every hour. This shows that he would cover 40 mi in 40 ÷ 10 = 4 h.

50 × 4 = 200 mi

He drove a distance of 200 mi.

11. (a) p km ⟶ 1 h

1 km ⟶ $\frac{1}{p}$ h

q km ⟶ $\frac{1}{p} × q = \frac{q}{p}$ h

He needs $\frac{q}{p}$ h to cycle q km.

(b) 1 h ⟶ t km (walk)

3 h ⟶ 3 × t = 3t km

1 h ⟶ p km

5 h ⟶ 5 × p = 5p km

3t km + 5p km = (3t + 5p) km

The total distance traveled is (3t + 5p) km.

Challenging Problems (pp. 64–68)

1.

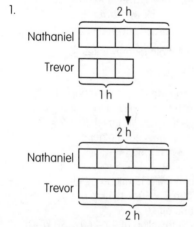

From the model, the ratio of Nathaniel's average speed to Trevor's average speed is 5 : 6.

2.

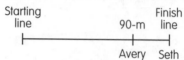

100 m/s

100 m

The full length of the train will be inside the tunnel after 1 s, and the train will be completely out of the tunnel after another 1 s.

1 s + 1 s = 2 s

It will take the train 2 s to pass completely through the tunnel.

3. Let the time taken by Seth be x minutes.

Using the same length of time (x minutes), Seth will reach the 90-m mark at the same time as Avery.

Starting line ——— Finish line

90-m line

10 m   Seth, Avery

Because Seth's speed is faster than Avery's, he can run the last 10 m in a shorter time as compared to Avery. So, Seth will win the second race.

4.

Time: $7\frac{1}{10}$ h, Distance: 470 km

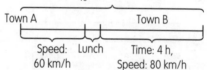

Town A   Town B

Speed: 60 km/h   Lunch   Time: 4 h, Speed: 80 km/h

Distance traveled after taking lunch = 80 × 4

$$= 320 \text{ km}$$

Distance traveled during first part of the journey = 470 km − 320 km

$$= 150 \text{ km}$$

Time taken for first part of the journey = 150 ÷ 60

$$= \frac{5}{2} \text{ h}$$

$$= 2\frac{1}{2} \text{ h}$$

$7\frac{1}{10}$ h − $2\frac{1}{2}$ h − 4 h = $7\frac{1}{10}$ h − $6\frac{1}{2}$ h

$$= \frac{3}{5} \text{ h}$$

$$= 36 \text{ min}$$

She took 36 min to have lunch.

5. Charles   passed   Timothy
   9:00 a.m.   each other   10:00 a.m.
   to noon   at noon   to noon

3 units   6 units

Town P   Town Q

270 mi

9 units → 270 mi
3 units → 270 ÷ 3 = 90 mi
(distance Charles travels)

Charles's average speed = 90 ÷ 3
= 30 mph

Distance Timothy travels = 270 − 90
= 180 mi

Timothy's average speed = 180 ÷ 2
= 90 mph

Charles's average speed is 30 mph and Timothy's average speed is 90 mph.

6. Since Arianna passed by Luis two times, she did it at the $\frac{1}{3}$-mark and $\frac{2}{3}$-mark along the track.

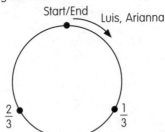

Start/End
Luis, Arianna
$\frac{2}{3}$
$\frac{1}{3}$

	Track		
Luis	$\frac{1}{3}$	$\frac{2}{3}$	$\frac{3}{3} = 1$
Arianna	$\frac{4}{3} = 1\frac{1}{3}$	$\frac{8}{3} = 2\frac{2}{3}$	$\frac{12}{3} = 4$

Arianna's running speed
= 4 × Luis's walking speed

If Arianna runs in the opposite direction, she will cover 4 times the distance Luis covers.

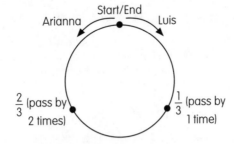

Arianna
Start/End
Luis
$\frac{2}{3}$ (pass by 2 times)
$\frac{1}{3}$ (pass by 1 time)

1 + 2 + 1 = 4 times

Arianna will pass by Luis 4 times if she runs around the track in the opposite direction.

7. Gabrielle spent $\frac{1}{6}$ of Paige's traveling time resting.

Paige spent $\frac{1}{5}$ of Gabrielle's traveling time resting.

Let the time taken by Gabrielle be x h and the time taken by Paige be y h.

x + Gabrielle's resting time
= y + Paige's resting time

$x + \frac{1}{6}y = y + \frac{1}{5}x$

$\frac{4}{5}x = \frac{5}{6}y$

$\frac{x}{y} = \frac{5}{6} \div \frac{4}{5}$

$= \frac{5}{6} \times \frac{5}{4}$

$= \frac{25}{24}$

Since the ratio of the time taken by Gabrielle to Paige is 25 : 24, the ratio of Gabrielle speed to Paige's speed is 24 : 25. (The shorter the time taken, the faster the speed.)

8. If the driver takes t h while traveling at v km/h and t_1 h while traveling at v_1 km/h,

$t : t_1 = 100 : (100 − 12.5)$
$= 100 : 87.5$
$= 200 : 175$
$= 8 : 7$

Since $t : t_1 = 8 : 7$, $v : v_1 = 7 : 8$ (the longer the time taken, the slower the speed).

1 unit → 10 km/h
7 units → 70 km/h

The driver drove at 70 km/h from Town A to Town B.

9. Length of time between 7:00 a.m. to 3:00 p.m. = 8 h

8 h + 5 h = 13 h

Let the speed of Car S be V_s and the speed of Car T be V_t.

Since the distance traveled by both cars is the same,

$13V_s − 13V_t = 150$

$V_s − V_t = \frac{150}{13}$

$5V_s = 8V_t$

$V_s = \frac{8}{5}V_t$

$\frac{8}{5}V_t − V_t = \frac{150}{13}$

$\frac{3}{5}V_t = \frac{150}{13}$

$V_t = \frac{150}{13} \times \frac{5}{3}$

$= \frac{250}{13}$

Distance between Town X and Town Y

$= \frac{250}{13} \times 13 + 150$

$= 400$ km

The distance between Town X and Town Y was 400 km.

10. Carter's speed = 36 m/min
Ian's speed = 42 m/min
Jaden's speed = 48 m/min
Let Ian and Jaden meet each other after
t min.

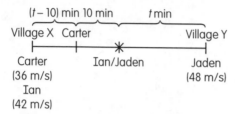

Distance between Village X and Village Y
= distance traveled by Ian and Jaden up
  till when they passed by each other
= $42t + 48t$
= $90t$
Distance traveled by Ian when he passed
by Jaden = $42t$
Distance traveled by Ian when he passed
by Jaden
= distance traveled by Carter + distance
  traveled by Jaden from the time he
  passed by Ian to the time he passed
  by Carter
$42t = 36(t - 10) + 48 \times 10$
$42t = 36t - 360 + 480$
$42t = 36t + 120$
$6t = 120$
$t = 120 \div 6$
$\quad = 20$
$90t = 90 \times 20$
$\quad = 1800$ m
$\quad = 1.8$ km
The distance between the two villages was
1.8 km.

6 Circles

Practice Questions (pp. 70–74)

1.
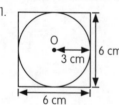

36 cm^2 = 6 cm $\times$ 6 cm
Length of one side of square = 6 cm
Radius of circle = 6 cm $\div$ 2
$\quad = 3$ cm
Area of circle = $\pi \times 3$ cm $\times 3$ cm
$\quad = 9\pi$ cm^2
The area of the circle is 9π cm^2.

2. Area of shaded part
= area of big circle – area of small circle
= $(\pi \times 3$ units $\times 3$ units$) - (\pi \times 2$ units $\times 2$ units$)$
= 9π sq units $- 4\pi$ sq units
= 5π sq units^2
The area of the shaded part is 5π sq units.

3.
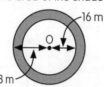

Area of pathway
= area of big circle – area of small circle
= $(\pi \times 18$ m $\times 18$ m$) - (\pi \times 16$ m $\times 16$ m$)$
= 324π m$^2 - 256\pi$ m^2
= 68π m^2
The area of the pathway is 68π m^2.

4. Length of belt needed
= circumference of one circular pulley
  $+ 2 \times 4 \times$ radius of one circular pulley
= $(2 \times \dfrac{22}{7} \times 7$ cm$) + (2 \times 4 \times 7$ cm$)$
= 44 cm $+ 56$ cm
= 100 cm
The length of belt needed to enclose the
pulleys is 100 cm.

5. In square OBEC, BC = OE
$\qquad\qquad\qquad\quad$ = radius of OCD
$\qquad\qquad\qquad\quad$ = 7 cm
The distance from B to C is 7 cm.

6.
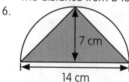

Greatest possible area = $\dfrac{1}{2} \times 14$ cm $\times 7$ cm
$\qquad\qquad\qquad\qquad = 49$ cm^2
The greatest possible area of a triangle that
can be drawn in the semicircle is 49 cm^2.

7.
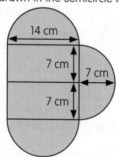

Area of figure
= area of 2 rectangles + area of
  3 semicircles
= (2 × 14 cm × 7 cm)
  + $(3 × \frac{1}{2} × \frac{22}{7} × 7 \text{ cm} × 7 \text{ cm})$
= 196 cm² + 231 cm²
= 427 cm²
The area of the figure is 427 cm².

8. Let the cost of a regular pizza be $10.50.
   So, the cost of a large pizza will be
   2 × $10.50 = $21.00.
   Area of a regular pizza = πr^2 cm²
   Area of a large pizza = $\pi(\frac{3}{2}r)^2$
   $\qquad\qquad = \frac{9}{4}\pi r^2$ cm²
   πr^2 = $10.50 (regular)
   $2\pi r^2$ = $21 (2 regular)
   $\frac{9}{4}\pi r^2$ = $21
   $\frac{9}{4}\pi r^2 > 2\pi r^2$
   It costs less per sq unit for the large pizza.
   It is a better deal to buy one large pizza.

9.

   Area of shaded part
   = area of square – area of 4 circles
   = (2 × 2 × 3 cm × 2 × 2 × 3 cm)
     – (4 × π × 3 cm × 3 cm)
   = (144 – 36π) cm²
   The area of the shaded part is (144 – 36π) cm².

10. Total area of shapes removed
    = total area of 3 quarter circles + area of
      2-cm square
    = $3 × \frac{1}{4} × \pi × 2\text{cm} × 2\text{cm} + 2\text{cm} × 2\text{cm}$
    = (3π + 4) cm²
    Area of figure
    = area of square – total area of shapes
      removed
    = 9 × 9 cm – (3π + 4) cm²
    = (81 – 3π – 4) cm²
    = (77 – 3π) cm²
    The area of the figure is (77 – 3π) cm².

Challenging Problems (pp. 76–80)

1. The second wheel makes 1 complete turn
   after moving around half the circumference
   of the fixed wheel. So, it make 2 complete
   turns after moving 1 complete turn around
   the fixed wheel. (Try it out with two actual
   wheels.)

2.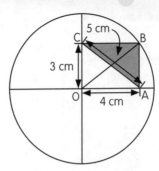

   AC = OB
   $\quad$ = radius of circle
   $\quad$ = 5 cm
   Area of shaded part = $\frac{1}{2}$ × 3 cm × 4 cm
   $\qquad\qquad\qquad$ = 6 cm²
   Area of circle = π × 5 cm × 5 cm
   $\qquad\qquad$ = 25π cm²
   $\frac{6}{25\pi}$ of the circle is shaded.

3. If r is the radius of the big circle, then the
   radius of each of the small circles is $\frac{r}{2}$.
   Area of big circle = πr^2 cm²
   Area of each small circle = $\pi\left(\frac{r}{2}\right)^2$
   $\qquad\qquad\qquad\qquad = \frac{\pi r^2}{4}$ cm²
   Area of shaded part
   = Area of two small circles
   = $2 × \frac{\pi r^2}{4}$ cm²
   = $\frac{1}{2}\pi r^2$ cm²
   $\frac{1}{2}$ of the big circle is shaded.

4. Perimeter of tray
   = sum of circumference of 3 $\frac{1}{3}$-circle
     + 3 × 2 × radius of circle
   = $(3 × \frac{1}{3} × 2 × \frac{22}{7} × 7 \text{ in.}) + (3 × 2 × 7 \text{ in.})$
   = 44 in. + 42 in.
   = 86 in.
   The perimeter of the tray is 86 in.

5.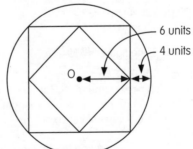

   The radius of the circle = 6 + 4 = 10 units.
   XY = OZ = radius of circle
   This is also the length of one side of the
   rhombus.

Perimeter of rhombus = 4 × 10
= 40 units
The perimeter of the rhombus is 40 units.

6.

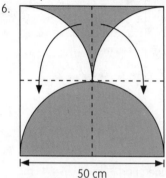

50 cm

Total area of shaded parts
= area of rectangle
$= 50 \text{ cm} \times (\frac{1}{2} \times 50 \text{ cm})$
= 50 cm × 25 cm
= 1250 cm²
The total area of the shaded parts is
1250 cm².

7. Length of each side of square
= 2 × radius of quarter circle
= 2 × 5 cm
= 10 cm
Area of shaded part
= area of square − area of 3 quarter circles
+ area of 3 quarter circles
= area of square
= 10 cm × 10 cm
= 100 cm²
The area of the shaded part is 100 cm².

8. Area of figure
= area of 2 quarter circles + area of rectangle
+ area of 2 semicircles
= area of semicircle + area of rectangle +
area of circle
$= [\frac{1}{2} \times \frac{22}{7} \times (14 \text{ cm} \div 2) \times (14 \text{ cm} \div 2)] +$
$(21 \text{ cm} \times 14 \text{ cm}) + [\frac{22}{7} \times (14 \text{ cm} \div 2 \div 2) \times$
$(14 \text{ cm} \div 2 \div 2)]$
$= 77 \text{ cm}^2 + 294 \text{ cm}^2 + 38\frac{1}{2} \text{ cm}^2$
$= 409\frac{1}{2} \text{ cm}^2$
The area of the figure is $409\frac{1}{2}$ cm².

Perimeter of figure
= circumference of 2 quarter circles +
2 × radius of quarter circle + 2 × length
of rectangle + circumference of 2
semicircles
= circumference of semicircle + 2 × radius
of quarter circle + 2 × length of rectangle
+ circumference of circle

$= [\frac{1}{2} \times 2 \times \frac{22}{7} \times (14 \text{ cm} \div 2)] +$
$[2 \times (14 \text{ cm} \div 2)] + (2 \times 21 \text{ cm}) + [2 \times \frac{22}{7} \times$
$(14 \text{ cm} \div 2)]$
= 22 cm + 14 cm + 42 cm + 44 cm
= 122 cm
The perimeter of the figure is 122 cm.

9.

D ——————————— C
Y
Z   Z
X
A ——————————— B
14 m

Let the area of the unshaded part on either
side of X be z.
Area of shaded part X
− area of shaded part Y
= area of part (X + z) − area of part (Y + z)
= area of quarter circle − area of semicircle
− (area of square − area of quarter circle)
$= (\frac{1}{4} \times \frac{22}{7} \times 14 \text{ m} \times 14 \text{ m} - \frac{1}{2} \times \frac{22}{7} \times 7 \text{ m}$
$\times 7 \text{ m}) - (14 \text{ m} \times 14 \text{ m} - \frac{1}{4} \times \frac{22}{7} \times 14 \text{ m}$
$\times 14 \text{ m})$
= (154 − 77) m² − (196 − 154) m²
= 77 m² − 42 m²
= 35 m²
The difference between the area of the
shaded part X and the shaded part Y is
35 m².

10. Let the radius of Circle P be r. Then the
radius of Circle Q is 8r.
Area of shaded part
= area of Circle Q − area of Circle P
= (π × 8r cm × 8r cm) − (π × r cm × r cm)
= 64πr² cm² − πr² cm²
= 63πr² cm²
63πr² = 9702
r² = 9702 ÷ 63π
$= 9702 \div (63 \times \frac{22}{7})$
= 49
= 7 × 7
r = 7 cm
Circumference of Circle Q = 2π × (8 × 7 cm)
= 112π cm
Circumference of Circle P = 2π × 7 cm
= 14π cm

Difference in circumference
$= 112\pi \text{ cm} - 14\pi \text{ cm}$
$= 98\pi \text{ cm}$
$= (98 \times \dfrac{22}{7}) \text{ cm}$
$= 308 \text{ cm}$
The difference in the circumference of the two circles is 308 cm.

7 Volume

Practice Questions (pp. 82–86)

1. (a)

Number of 12-cm³ glasses	Volume of sand	Number of 15-cm³ glassess	Volume of sand
1	12	1	15
2	24	2	30
3	36	3	45
4	48	4	**60**
5	**60**	5	75

Eve poured five 12-cm³ glasses of sand into the container. Adam poured four 15-cm³ glasses of sand.

(b) $60 \text{ cm}^3 + 60 \text{ cm}^3 = 120 \text{ cm}^3$
The volume of sand in the container is 120 cm³.

2. Volume of water in Container Y
$= 5 \text{ ft.} \times 6 \text{ ft.} \times 12 \text{ ft.}$
$= 360 \text{ ft.}^3$

Container X

360 ft.³

3 units $\longrightarrow$ 360 ft.³
1 unit $\longrightarrow$ 360 ft.³ ÷ 3 = 120 ft.³
5 units $\longrightarrow$ 5 × 120 ft.³ = 600 ft.³
The volume of water in Container X was 600 ft.³ at first.

3. (a) 1 plastic container + 2 bottles
$= 960 \text{ ml (given)}$
2 plastic containers + 4 bottles
$= 2 \times 960 \text{ ml}$
$= 1920 \text{ ml}$
2 plastic containers + 1 bottle
$= 870 \text{ ml (given)}$
4 bottles – 1 bottle = 1920 ml – 870 ml
$= 1050 \text{ ml}$
3 bottles = 1050 ml
1 bottle = 1050 ml ÷ 3
$= 350 \text{ ml}$
The capacity of one bottle is 350 ml.

(b) 2 bottles = 2 × 350 ml
$= 700 \text{ ml}$
1 plastic container + 700 ml = 960 ml
1 plastic container = 960 ml – 700 ml
$= 260 \text{ ml}$
The capacity of one plastic container is 260 ml.

4. Volume of wooden block = 9 m × 15 m × 6 m
$= 810 \text{ m}^3$
Total volume of square holes
$= 3 \text{ m} \times 3 \text{ m} \times 15 \text{ m} + 2 \text{ m} \times 2 \text{ m} \times 15 \text{ m}$
$= 135 \text{ m}^3 + 60 \text{ m}^3$
$= 195 \text{ m}^3$
Volume of remaining wooden block
$= 810 \text{ m}^3 - 195 \text{ m}^3$
$= 615 \text{ m}^3$
The volume of the remaining wooden block is 615 m³.

5. (a) $\dfrac{1}{2} \times 3 \text{ cm} \times 4 \text{ cm} \times 8 \text{ cm} = 48 \text{ cm}^3$

(b) $\dfrac{1}{2} \times (3 \text{ cm} + 5 \text{ cm}) \times 2 \text{ cm} \times 12 \text{ cm} = 96 \text{ cm}^3$

6. Volume of water it can hold when full
$= \dfrac{1}{2} \times \dfrac{22}{7} \times 14 \text{ cm} \times 14 \text{ cm} \times 500 \text{ cm}$
$= 154{,}000 \text{ cm}^3$
It can hold 154,000 cm³ of water when full.

7. Time taken
$= (500 \text{ cm} \times 300 \text{ cm} \times 200 \text{ cm}) \div 3{,}000 \text{ cm}^3$
$= 10{,}000 \text{ s}$
$\approx 167 \text{ min}$
It took the pipe about 167 min to fill up the tank.

8. Volume of metal dumbbell
$=$ volume of 2 wheels + volume of rod
$= 2 \times (3.14 \times 4 \text{ in.} \times 4 \text{ in.} \times 3 \text{ in.}) + (3.14 \times 1 \text{ in.} \times 1 \text{ in.} \times 8 \text{ in.})$
$= (301.44 + 25.12) \text{ in.}^3$
$= 326.56 \text{ in.}^3$
The volume of the metal dumbbell is 326.56 in.³.

9. Volume of metal cube = 12 ft. × 12 ft. × 12 ft.
$= 1728 \text{ ft.}^3$
Rise in water level
$= (12 \text{ ft.} \times 12 \text{ ft.} \times 12 \text{ ft.}) \div (24 \text{ ft.} \times 20 \text{ ft.})$
$= 1728 \text{ ft.}^3 \div 480 \text{ ft.}^2$
$= 3.6 \text{ ft.}$
New height of water level = 16 ft. + 3.6 ft.
$= 19.6 \text{ ft.}$
The new height of the water level is 19.6 ft.

10. 11.4 l = 11,400 cm³
Height of water level
$= 11{,}400 \text{ cm}^3 \div (60 \text{ cm} \times 20 \text{ cm})$
$= 9.5 \text{ cm}$
Initial water level = 23.9 cm – 9.5 cm
$= 14.4 \text{ cm}$

$\frac{2}{5}$ of height of container ⟶ 14.4 cm

$\frac{1}{5}$ of height of container ⟶ 14.4 cm ÷ 2
= 7.2 cm

$\frac{5}{5}$ of height of container ⟶ 5 × 7.2 cm
= 36 cm

The height of the container was 36 cm.

Challenging Problems (pp. 88–93)

1. Volume of water in Container P
= $\frac{2}{3}$ × 75 cm × 40 cm × 120 cm
= 240,000 cm³

Imagine placing the two containers next to each other.

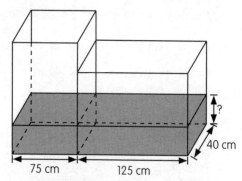

Let h cm be the height of the water level in each container.

(75 cm + 125 cm) × 40 cm × h cm
= 240,000 cm³

200 cm × 40 cm × h cm = 240,000 cm³
8000h cm³ = 240,000 cm³
h = 240,000 cm³ ÷ 8000 cm²
= 30 cm

The height of the water level in each container is 30 cm.

2.

Tank P

30 cm³

Tank Q

50 cm³

Tank P

Tank Q

4 units + 5 × 30 cm³ = 3 units + 4 × 50 cm³
4 units + 150 cm³ = 3 units + 200 cm³
4 units − 3 units = 200 cm³ − 150 cm³
1 unit = 50 cm³

Tank Q = 3 units + 4 × 50 cm³
= 3 × 50 cm³ + 200 cm³
= 150 cm³ + 200 cm³
= 350 cm³

The volume of water in Tank Q now is 350 cm³.

3. Before

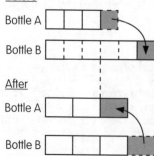

Bottle A

Bottle B

After

Bottle A

Bottle B

From the model, we can see that the ratio of the initial volume of water in Bottle A to the initial volume of water in Bottle B is 4 : 5.

4. Since 512 cm³ = 8 cm × 8 cm × 8 cm, the length of one edge of Cube A is 8 cm.
Length of one edge of Cube B
= 8 cm + 4 cm + 4 cm
= 16 cm

Volume of Cube B = 16 cm × 16 cm × 16 cm
= 4096 cm³

Volume of solid
= volume of Cube A + volume of Cube B
= 512 cm³ + 4096 cm³
= 4608 cm³

The volume of the solid is 4608 cm³.

5. Volume of figure
= [(24 cm × 12 cm) − ($\frac{1}{2}$ × 10 cm × 10 cm)
+ (35 cm × 6 cm)] × 10 cm
= [(288 − 157 + 210) × 10] cm³
= (341 × 10) cm³
= 3410 cm³

The volume of the figure is 3410 cm³.

6. Volume of water flowing through the pipe in 1 min = (2.5 × 100 × 100 × 100) cm³
Height of water level
= (2.5 × 100 cm × 100 cm × 100 cm)
÷ ($\frac{22}{7}$ × 42 cm × 42 cm)
= 450.9 cm
≈ 451

The height of the water level in the tank after one minute is about 451 cm.

7. Capacity of tank = 60 cm × 35 cm × 45 cm
= 94,500 cm³

Volume of water needed to fill up the tank
= 94,500 cm³ − 7500 cm³
= 87,000 cm³

Time taken to fill tank to its brim
= 87,000 cm^3 ÷ (12 × 1000) min
= 7.25 min
It will take 7.25 min to fill the tank to its brim.

8. Total volume of solid and water in the tank
= 60 cm × 40 cm × 24 cm
= 57,600 cm^3
Total volume of water that flowed into the tank after 3.5 min = 3.5 × (9 × 1000 cm^3)
= 31,500 cm^3
Volume of solid
= 57,600 cm^3 − 31,500 cm^3
= 26,100 cm^3
The volume of the solid is 26,100 cm^3.

9. Capacity of rectangular tank
= 12 cm × 15 cm × 18 cm
= 3240 cm^3
Total volume of metal block and water in the tank = $\frac{2}{5}$ × 3240 cm^3
= 1296 cm^3
Volume of water in the tank
= 1296 cm^3 − 196 cm^3
= 1100 cm^3
Volume of water needed to fill the tank
= 3240 cm^3 − 1296 cm^3
= 1944 cm^3
1100 cm^3 → 11 min
1944 cm^3 → $\frac{11}{1100}$ × 1944 = 19.44 min
It will take 19.44 min to fill the tank completely.

10. Capacity of container
= 80 cm × 60 cm × 30 cm
= 144,000 cm^3
Rate of water flowing from Tap P
= 144,000 cm^3 ÷ 8
= 18,000 cm^3 per minute
= 18 l per minute
Rate of water flowing from Tap Q
= 144,000 cm^3 ÷ 12
= 12,000 cm^3 per minute
= 12 l per minute
(a) Total rate of water flowing into the container = 18 l + 12 l
= 30 l per min
The total rate of water flowing into the container is 30 l per minute.
(b) Time taken for both taps to fill the container with water
= 144,000 cm^3 ÷ 30,000 cm^3
= 4.8 min
It will take 4.8 min for them to fill the container with water.

8 Data Analysis

Practice Questions (pp. 95–101)

1. The runner who took the longest time to complete the race is the last.

Runner	Time taken (in s)	Position
Dave	14.3	1st
Carl	14.4	2nd
Emmanuel	15.2	3rd
Alvin	15.7	4th
Bobby	15.8	5th

(a) Dave came in first.
(b) Bobby came in last.
(c) Difference in time taken by the first and last runner = 15.8 s − 14.3 s
= 1.5 s
The range is 1.5 s.
(d) (14.3 s + 14.4 s + 15.2 s + 15.7 s + 15.8 s) ÷ 5 = 15.08 s
The mean time taken by the 5 runners is 15.08 s.

2.

Height of young shoot (in cm)				
56	60	78	86	110

Median = height of young shoot 3
The median height of the young shoots is 78 cm.

3.

PSI reading													
10	15	20	25	30	35	40	45	50	55	60	65	70	85

Median = average of 40 and 45
= (40 + 45) ÷ 2
= 42.5
The median PSI reading is 42.5.

4. Since there are 120 members (an even number of data), the median age is the average of the middle 2 members.

10–29 years	30–39 years	40–49 years	50–59 years
57	30	25	8

Median age = average age of 60th and 61st member
= (30 years + 30 years) ÷ 2
= 30 years
The median age of the members is 30 years.

5. The highest score is 92.
The lowest score is 51.
The range of scores is the difference between the highest and the lowest score, which is 92 − 51 = 41.

6. (a) The plant grew from 150 mm to 220 mm
between the 2nd and 4th week.
(220 mm – 150 mm) ÷ 14 = 5 mm
The mean growth of the plant was
5 mm each day.
   (b) The plant grew from 40 mm to 240 mm
over the period of 5 weeks.
(240 mm – 40 mm) ÷ 5 = 40 mm
The mean growth of the plant over the
5 weeks was 40 mm.

7. (a) A score of 69 occurs most frequently.
The mode is 69.
   (b)

Test	2	5	8	6	1	4	3	7
Score	69	69	69	70	73	81	87	90

Median = average of 70 and 73
= (70 + 73) ÷ 2
= 71.5
The median score is 71.5.
   (c) Mean = (73 + 69 + 87 + 81 + 69 + 70
+ 90 + 69) ÷ 8
= 76
The mean score is 76.

8. (a) Mean
= ($2080 + $3400 + $1950 + $2500
+ $1600 + $2100 + $2200 + $1730
+ $2750 + $3020 + $4600 + $3000
+ $3160 + $2650 + $3350 + $1880
+ $2180 + $1980 + $2000 + $2080
+ $2810 + $2170 + $1840 + $2300
+ $3090 + $2930 + $3140 + $2220
+ $2380 + $3260) ÷ 30
= $2545
The mean toll collected along the
highway in June is $2545.
   (b) Mean = ($1950 + $1600 + $1730 + $1880
+ $1840) ÷ 5
= $1800
The mean toll collected in this sample
is $1800.

9. (a) Travel + Sports + Meal = $\frac{1}{2}$ of pie chart

1.5 h + 3 h + 2.5 h = 7 h

Travel + School = $\frac{1}{2}$ of pie chart

1.5 h + Time he spends in school
= 7 h
Time he spends in school = 7 h – 1.5 h
= 5.5 h
Noah spends 5.5 h in school.
   (b) $\frac{1}{2}$ of the pie chart represents 1.5 h + 3 h
+ 2.5 h = 7 h.
The pie chart represents 2 × 7 h = 14 h.

$\frac{1.5}{14} = \frac{15}{140}$
$= \frac{3}{28}$

He spends $\frac{3}{28}$ of his time traveling.

10. (a) Median amount of money collected
= average of amount collected by
30th and 31st student
= ($35 + $35) ÷ 2
= $35
The median amount of money collected
was $35.
   (b) From the graph, we can see that the
median amount of money collected lies
in the $30–$39 range.

Challenging Problems (pp. 104–110)

1. The sum of the numbers in Group X is 41.
The sum of the numbers in Group Y is 49.
The sum of the numbers in both groups
is 41 + 49 = 90.
So, their mean is 90 ÷ 9 = 10.
The sum of the 4 numbers in Group X
must be 4 × 10 = 40, and the sum of the
5 numbers in Group Y must be
5 × 10 = 50.
Group X needs 1 less and Group Y needs
1 more.
The number 14 from Group X must be
switched with the number 13 from
Group Y so that both groups will have
the same mean.

2. The sum of 10, 7, 9, 12, and 6 is 44.
A multiple of 7 greater than but close to 44
is 49, which means $p + q$ has a value of 5.
If $p + q = 5$, then the mean = $\frac{49}{7}$ = 7
= median.

p	q	6	7	9	10	12

So, p and q can be 1 and 4, or 2 and 3
respectively.

3. $\underline{5}$ $\underline{}$ $\underline{}$ $\underline{}$ $\underline{}$ $\underline{31}$
The sum of the 6 numbers is 6 × 16 = 96.
Since the range is 26, the first number is
31 – 26 = 5.
Since the median is 15, the sum of the third
and fourth number is 2 × 15 = 30.
The third and fourth number could be 9 and
21 or 11 and 19, so the second number could
be 7 or 9.
The greatest possible value for the second
number is 9.

4. Accept any possible answers:

	1st number	2nd number	3rd number	4th number	5th number	6th number
Possible set 1	4	4	4	4	4	4
Possible set 2	1	1	1	7	7	7
Possible set 3	1	1	1	1	1	19
Possible set 4	0	1	2	3	4	14
⋮	⋮	⋮	⋮	⋮	⋮	⋮

5. (a) Arranging the cab drivers' earnings in order, we obtain the following table:

Earnings				
$83	$85	$87	$88	$92
$95	$97	$101	$102	$103
$110	$110	$117	$117	$120
$121	$123	$123	$124	$130
$130	$132	$135	$145	

Median earnings
= average of 12th and 13th cab driver's earnings
= ($110 + $117) ÷ 2
= $113.50
The mean earnings is $113.50.

(b) Arranging the cab drivers' earnings in order, we obtain the following table:

Earnings				
$83	$85	$87	$88	$92
$95	$97	$100	$101	$102
$103	$110	$110	$117	$117
$120	$121	$123	$123	$124
$130	$130	$132	$135	$145

Median earnings = 13th cab driver's earnings
= $110
The new median earnings is $110.

6. (a) $\frac{54}{360} \times 100\% = 15\%$
15% of the people who attended the computer fair were girls.

(b)

Men	Women
x	$2x$

$x° + 2x° = 360° - 54° - 81°$
$= 225°$
$3x° = 225°$
$x = \frac{225}{3}$
$= 75$
The value of x is 75.

(c) 54° represents 324 people.
1° represents 324 ÷ 54 = 6 people.
360° represents 360 × 6 = 2160 people.
2160 people attended the computer fair.

7. (a)

	Jeremiah	Erin	Carlos
	Working hours		
April	176	170	190
May	176	180	190
June	162	180	194
Total	514	530	574

(514 h + 530 h + 574 h) ÷ 3 = 539.33 h
≈ 539 h
The average number of hours that Jeremiah, Erin, and Carlos worked from April to June was about 539 hours.

(b)

	Jeremiah	Erin	Carlos
Working hours	170	190	198
Wage	75 × $7 + (170 − 75) × $9 = $1380	65 × $6 + (190 − 65) × $8 = $1390	100 × $5 + (198 − 100) × $8 = $1284

($1380 + $1390 + $1284) ÷ 3 = $1351.33
≈ $1351
Their average wage in July was about $1351.

8. (a) Percentage of people who are children
= 100% − 40% − 25% − 8%
= 27%
$\frac{27}{100} \times 2400 = 648$
There are 648 children at the country club.

(b) Percentage of people who are members
= 100% − 8%
= 92%

Members	:	Guests
= 92	:	8
= 23	:	2

The ratio of the number of members to the number of guests is 23 : 2.

(c) Number of children who are boys
$= \frac{75}{100} \times 648$
= 486
Number of men who are members
$= \frac{40}{100} \times 2400$
= 960
Number of male members
= 486 boys + 960 men
= 1446

Number of members
$$= \frac{92}{100} \times 2400$$
$$= 2208$$
$$\frac{1446}{2208} \times 100\% = 65.49\%$$
$$\approx 65\%$$
About 65% of the members are male.

9. (a) Mean weight
$$= (2 \times 1.5 \text{ kg} + 2 \times 2 \text{ kg} + 4 \times 2.5 \text{ kg}$$
$$+ 3 \times 3 \text{ kg} + 2 \times 3.5 \text{ kg}) \div 11$$
$$= 33 \text{ kg} \div 11$$
$$= 3 \text{ kg}$$
The mean weight of the aquariums is 3 kg.

(b) Median weight = Weight of 6th aquarium
$$= 2.5 \text{ kg}$$
The median weight of the aquarium is 2.5 kg.

(c) New mean weight
$$= (11 \times 3 \text{ kg} + 2 \times 2 \text{ kg} + 1 \times 3 \text{ kg}$$
$$+ 2 \times 3.5 \text{ kg}) \div (11 + 5)$$
$$= 47 \text{ kg} \div 16$$
$$= 2.93 \text{ kg}$$
$$\approx 3 \text{ kg}$$
The new mean weight of the aquarium is 3 kg.
New median weight
= average of 8th and 9th aquarium
$$= (2.5 \text{ kg} + 2.5 \text{ kg}) \div 2$$
$$= 2.5 \text{ kg}$$
The new median weight of the aquarium is 2.5 kg.

10. (a) $\frac{1}{2} - \frac{1}{6} = \frac{3}{6} - \frac{1}{6}$
$$= \frac{2}{6}$$
$\frac{2}{6}$ of the pie chart represents 240 fruits.
$\frac{1}{6}$ of the pie chart represents
$240 \div 2 = 120$ fruits.
120 bananas were sold.

(b) $\frac{1}{2} - \frac{1}{8} = \frac{4}{8} - \frac{1}{8}$
$$= \frac{3}{8}$$
$\frac{1}{8}$ of the pie chart represents
$\frac{1}{8} \times (6 \times 120) = 90$ fruits.
$\frac{3}{8}$ of the pie chart represents
$3 \times 90 = 270$ fruits.
Number of oranges = Number of apples
$$= 270 \div 2$$
$$= 135$$

$135 - 90 = 45$
The difference between the number of apples and the number of kiwis sold is 45.

(c) Total number of fruits $= 6 \times 120$
$$= 720$$
$$\frac{135}{720} \times 100\% = 18.75\%$$
18.75% of the fruits sold were oranges.

(d) Number of oranges = 135
Amount earned from selling all oranges
$$= \$33.75$$
$$\$33.75 \div 135 = \$0.25$$
He earned $0.25 from selling each orange.

9 Angles

Practice Questions (pp. 113–117)

1. $\angle RQX = \angle SPZ$
$$= 42°$$
$\angle YPQ = \angle YQP$
$$= 90° - 42°$$
(complementary angles)
$$= 48°$$
$\angle PYQ = 180° - 48° - 48°$
(sum of angles in triangle)
$$= 84°$$
$\angle XYZ = \angle PYQ$
$$= 84°$$

2. $\angle ADB = 60°$ (equilateral triangle)
$\angle BDC = \angle DBC$
$$= 100° - 60°$$
$$= 40°$$
$\angle x = 180° - 40° - 40°$
(sum of angles in triangle)
$$= 100°$$

3. $\angle KNO = 90° - 52°$
(complementary angles)
$$= 38°$$
$\angle KON = 90° - 25°$
(complementary angles)
$$= 65°$$
$\angle p = 180° - 38° - 65°$
(sum of angles in triangle)
$$= 77°$$

4. $\angle SQR = 90° \div 2$
$$= 45°$$
$\angle RQY = 90° - 38°$ (complementary angles)
$$= 52°$$
$\angle SQY = 45° + 52°$
$$= 97°$$

5. $\angle ABC = \angle ACB$
(base angles of isosceles triangle)
$$= 75°$$
$\angle BAC = 180° - 75° - 75°$
(sum of angles in triangle)
$$= 30°$$

∠DAE = ∠BAC (isosceles triangle)
       = 30°
∠CAD = 180° − 30° − 30°
       (angles on a straight line)
       = 120°
∠ADY = (180° − 120°) ÷ 2
       (base angles of isosceles triangle)
       = 30°

6.

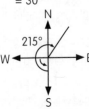

(a) 215° − 90° = 125°
    He turned through a total angle of 125°.
(b) 180° + (90° − 35°) = 180° + 55°
                    = 235°
    Or, 360° − 125° = 225°
    He must turn 235° in the clockwise
    direction in order to face West again.

7. ∠ABC = ∠EAB (equilateral triangle)
       = 60°
∠BFE = 180° − 60°
       (pair of angles between 2 parallel
       sides = 180°)
       = 120°
∠FBE = ∠FEB
       (base angles of isosceles triangle)
       = (180° − 120°) ÷ 2
       = 30°
∠EBA = 60° − 30°
       = 30°
∠BEA = 180° − ∠EAB − ∠EBA
       (sum of angles in triangle)
       = 180° − 60° − 30°
       = 90°
∠AEG = ∠BEA
       = 90°

8. ∠RBA = 180° − 48°
       (pair of angles between 2 parallel
       sides = 180°)
       = 132°
∠SBA = 180° − 132° (supplementary angles)
       = 48°
∠BAC = ∠CBA
       (base angles of isosceles triangle)
       = 48°
∠QAB = ∠QRB
       (opposite angles of parallelogram)
       = 48°
∠y = 180° − ∠QAB − ∠BAC
       (angles on a straight line)
       = 180° − 48° − 48°
       = 84°

9. **Method 1**
    360° ÷ 12 = 30°
    360° (minute-hand) ⟶ 30° (hour-hand)
               240° ⟶ $\frac{30}{360} \times 240° = 20°$
    The hour hand turns 20°.
Method 2
    360° ÷ 12 = 30°
    $\frac{240}{360} = \frac{2}{3}$
    $\frac{2}{3} \times 30° = 20°$
    The hour hand turns 20°.

10. ∠POW = ∠VOU (equilateral triangle)
           = ∠SOT
           = ∠ROQ
           = 60°
    ∠TOU = ∠VOW (angles at a point)
           = ∠POQ
           = ∠ROS
           = (360° − 4 × 60°) ÷ 4
           = 30°

Challenging Problems (pp. 119–124)

1. ∠SRO = ∠OSR
       (base angles of isosceles triangle)
       = 36°
∠SOR = 180° − 36° − 36°
       (sum of angles in triangle)
       = 108°
∠SOR = ∠POQ (isosceles triangle)
       = 108°
∠QOR + ∠POS = 360° − 108° − 108°
       (angles at a point)
       = 144°
$∠POS = \frac{1}{2}∠QOR$
∠QOR = 2∠POS
$∠QOR + \frac{1}{2}∠QOR = 144°$
$∠QOR = 144° \times \frac{2}{3}$
       = 96°
∠RQO = (180° − 96°) ÷ 2
       (base angles of isosceles triangle)
       = 42°

2. ∠RSQ = 180° − 62° − 78°
       (sum of angles in triangle)
       = 40°
∠SPQ = ∠QRS
       (opposite angles of parallelogram)
       = 62°
∠STP = ∠SPT
       (base angles of isosceles triangle)
       = 62°
∠PST = 180° − 62° − 62°
       (sum of angles in triangle)
       = 56°

∠RSP = 180° − 62°
        (pair of angles between 2 parallel
        sides = 180°)
    = 118°
∠y = 118° − 56° − 40°
    = 22°

3. ∠TSU = 180° − 32° (supplementary angles)
       = 148°
   ∠PQU = 180° − 148°
        (pair of angles between 2 parallel
        sides = 180°)
      = 32°
   ∠RUS = 180° − 32° − 66°
        (sum of angles in triangle)
      = 82°
   ∠QUP = ∠RUS (vertically opposite angles)
      = 82°
   ∠QPR = 180° − 32° − 82°
        (sum of angles in triangle)
      = 66°
   ∠PQR = ∠PRQ
        (base angles of isosceles triangle)
      = (180° − 66°) ÷ 2
      = 57°
   ∠x = 57° − ∠PQU
     = 57° − 32°
     = 25°

4. ∠RQV = 90° − 40° (complementary angles)
       = 50°
   ∠WRT = 180° − 135°
        (pair of angles between 2 parallel
        sides = 180°)
      = 45°
   ∠QRT = 90° − 45° (complementary angles)
       = 45°
   ∠QYR = 180° − 45° − 50°
        (sum of angles in triangle)
      = 85°
   ∠x = 180° − 85° (supplementary angles)
     = 95°

5. ∠AQB = 360° − 90° − 60° − 60°
        (angles at a point)
      = 150°
   ∠ABQ = (180° − 150°) ÷ 2
        (base angles of isosceles triangle)
      = 15°

6. ∠DCE = ∠CDE (equilateral triangle)
       = ∠CED
      = 60°
   ∠BCE = 90° − 60° (complementary angles)
      = 30°
   CD = BC
   ∠CBE = ∠CEB
        (base angles of isosceles triangle)
      = (180° − 30°) ÷ 2
      = 75°

∠DEA = ∠DAE
    = 75°
∠AEB = 360° − 2 × 75° − 60°
    (angles at a point)
    = 150°

7. ∠SPR = x°
       (base angles of isosceles triangle)
   ∠PSR = 180° − x° − x°
       (sum of angles in triangle)
      = 180° − 2x°
   ∠PSQ = 180° − (180° − 2x°)
       (sum of angles in triangle)
      = 2x°
   ∠QPS = ∠PQS
       (base angles of isosceles triangle)
      = (180° − 2x°) ÷ 2
      = 90° − x°
   ∠QPR = ∠QPS + x°
      = 90° − x° + x°
      = 90°

8. In ΔDBC, BD = CD.
   ∠DBC = ∠DCB
       (base angles of isosceles triangle)
      = (180° − 64°) ÷ 2
      = 58°
   In ΔADB, AD = BD.
   ∠ABD = ∠DAB
       (base angles of isosceles triangle)
      = (180° − 40°) ÷ 2
      = 70°
   ∠z = ∠ABD + ∠DBC
     = 70° + 58°
     = 128°
   In ΔADC,
   ∠DAC = ∠DCA
       (base angles of isosceles triangle)
      = (180° − 40° − 64°) ÷ 2
      = 38°
   ∠x = ∠DAB − ∠DAC
     = 70° − 38°
     = 32°
   ∠y = ∠DCB − ∠DCA
     = 58° − 38°
     = 20°

9. **Method 1**
   ∠SOQ = 180° − 150° (supplementary angles)
      = 30°
   ∠QOY = 90° − 30° (complementary angles)
      = 60°
   ∠a = 90° − 60° (complementary angles)
     = 30°
   Method 2
   ∠POX = 90°
   ∠a = 360° − 150° − 90° − 90°
      (angles at a point)
     = 30°

10. (a)

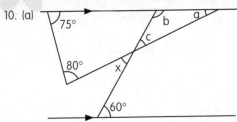

∠a = 180° − 75° − 80°
    (sum of angles in triangle)
   = 25°
∠b = 180° − 60° (supplementary angles)
   = 120°
∠x = ∠c (vertically opposite angles)
   = 180° − ∠a − ∠b
    (sum of angles in triangle)
   = 180° − 25° − 120°
   = 35°

(b)

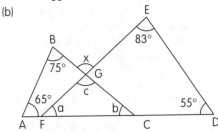

∠a = 180° − 83° − 55°
    (sum of angles in triangle)
   = 42°
∠b = 180° − 75° − 65°
    (sum of angles in triangle)
   = 40°
∠x = ∠c (vertically opposite angles)
   = 180° − ∠a + ∠b
    (sum of angles in a triangle)
   = 180° − 42° + 40°
   = 98°

10 Mixed Problems 1

Practice Questions (pp. 126–130)

1. 11 s

2.

Day	Number of coins
1st	1
2nd	2
3rd	4
4th	8
5th	16
6th	32
7th	64
8th	128
9th	256
10th	512

Since the piggy bank was full on the 10th day, it was half full the previous day (the number of coins in the piggy bank doubles each day).
Hence, the piggy bank was half full on the 9th day.

3. 161 = 7 × 23
'7' represents the number of hours each employee works each day and '23' represents the number of employees.
There are 23 employees.

4. Before

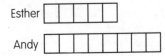

After

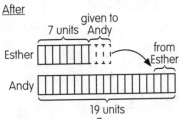

Esther's cards are $\frac{7}{19}$ of Andy's cards.

5. weight of pail

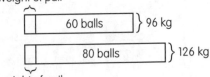

weight of pail

126 kg − 96 kg = 30 kg
20 balls weigh 30 kg.
60 balls weigh 3 × 30 kg = 90 kg.
96 kg − 90 kg = 6 kg
The weight of the empty pail is 6 kg.

6.

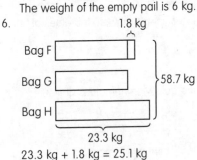

23.3 kg + 1.8 kg = 25.1 kg
58.7 kg − 25.1 kg = 33.6 kg
2 units → 33.6 kg
 1 unit → 33.6 kg ÷ 2 = 16.8 kg
1 unit + 1.8 kg = 16.8 kg + 1.8 kg
           = 18.6 kg
Bag F weighs 18.6 kg.

7. When Kaylee started saving, Henry had already saved 8 × $0.50 = $4.
Since Kaylee has saved $10 more than Henry now, she must have saved $10 + $4 = $14 more since she started saving.
So Kaylee must have taken $14 ÷ $0.20 = 1400 ÷ 20 = 70 days to save $14.
Her current savings is 70 × $0.70 = $49.

8.

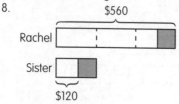

$560

Rachel

Sister

$120

2 [ ] → $560 − $120 − $120 − $120 = $200

1 [ ] → $200 ÷ 2 = $100

Their father gave each of them $100.

9. Pumpkins

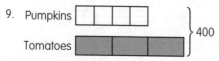

Tomatoes

400

After sale

1 [ ] + 1 [ ] = 120

4 [ ] + 4 [ ] = 4 × 120 = 480

4 [ ] + 3 [ ] = 400 (given)

1 [ ] → 480 − 400 = 80

3 [ ] → 3 × 80 = 240

Fraction of fruits that were tomatoes at first
$= \dfrac{240}{400}$
$= \dfrac{3}{5}$
$\dfrac{3}{5}$ of the fruits were tomatoes at first.

10.

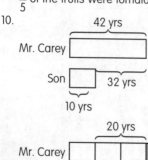

42 yrs

Mr. Carey

Son   32 yrs

10 yrs

20 yrs

Mr. Carey

Son   32 yrs

10 yrs

20 years + 2 [ ] = 32 years

2 [ ] → 32 years − 20 years = 12 years

1 [ ] → 12 years ÷ 2 = 6 years

Mr. Carey will be 3 times as old as his son in 6 years' time.

Challenging Problems (pp. 132–137)

1. The smaller number is 7.85 and the larger number is 13.04.
The product of the two decimals is 102.364.

2. The empty box weighs 20 g.
Each pin weighs 2 g.

3. (a) There were 7 students.
(b) Each student had 2 cups of tea and 1 piece of cake.

4. Since 429 = 3 × 11 × 13, there are either 13 schools, each sending 3 × 11 = 33 students or 11 schools, each sending 3 × 13 = 39 students.

5. From page 1 to 100, there are 11 pages with page numbers that contain the digit five and are also divisible by five. The same applies to pages 101 to 200, 201 to 300, and 301 to 400. From page 401 to 500, there 12 such pages.
Total number of pages = 4 × 11 + 12
                                    = 56
56 pages numbers contain the digit five and are also divisible by five.

6. Before

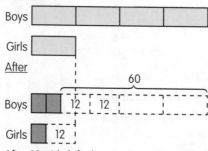

Boys

Girls

After

60

Boys   12   12

Girls   12

After 12 girls left, the number of boys left is

2 [ ], which is 2 [ ] + 12 + 12.

2 [ ] → 60 − 24 = 36

1 [ ] → 36 ÷ 2 = 18

4 [ ] → 4 × 18 = 72

There were 72 boys at first.

7. If Oliver lost 10 tokens to Jill

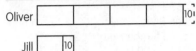

If Oliver lost 44 tokens to Jill

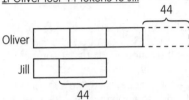

1 unit ⟶ 44 − 10 = 34
4 units + 10 ⟶ 4 × 34 + 10 = 146
Oliver had 146 tokens at first.

8.
Guavas [diagram] 260
Kiwis [diagram]

8 − 3 = 5 units
5 units ⟶ 260
1 unit ⟶ 260 ÷ 5 = 52
3 units ⟶ 3 × 52 = 156
156 guavas were sold.
156 ÷ 6 = 26
Each customer bought 26 guavas.

9. Area of region P
$= (\dfrac{\pi \times 3 \times 3}{2} - \dfrac{\pi \times 2 \times 2}{2} + \dfrac{\pi \times 1 \times 1}{2})$ cm²
$= 3\pi$ cm²
Area of region Q
$= [2 \times (\dfrac{\pi \times 2 \times 2}{2} - \dfrac{\pi \times 1 \times 1}{2})]$ cm²
$= 3\pi$ cm²
Area of region R = area of region P
$= 3\pi$ cm²
The ratio of the area of region P to the area of region Q to the area of region R is 1 : 1 : 1.

10. Diameter of each small circle = 6 cm
Radius of each small circle = 6 cm ÷ 2
$= 3$ cm
Area of 4 small circles = 4 × π × 3 cm × 3 cm
$= 36\pi$ cm²
Area of big circle = π × 12 cm × 12 cm
$= 144\pi$ cm²
Area of shaded part = 144π cm² − 36π cm²
$= 108\pi$ cm²

$\dfrac{36\pi}{108\pi} = \dfrac{1}{3}$

The total area of the four small circles is $\dfrac{1}{3}$ of the area of the shaded part.

11 Mixed Problems 2
Practice Questions (pp. 139–144)

1. 135 mi
2. 2 h
3. $\dfrac{1}{2}$
4. 132°
5. 56°
6. From 1st to 10th pole, there are 9 intervals.
From 1st to 16th pole, there are 15 intervals.
9 intervals take 6 min.
15 intervals take $\dfrac{6}{9} \times 15 = 10$ min.
It will take 10 minutes to reach the 16th pole.

7. Sum of 7 numbers = 7 × 8
$= 56$
Sum of 8 numbers = 8 × 9
$= 72$

72 − 56 = 16
The eighth number is 16.

8.

English	Math	Science
$\dfrac{50}{80} \times 100\%$	$\dfrac{80}{100} \times 100\%$	$\dfrac{100}{120} \times 100\%$
$= 62.5\%$	$= 80\%$	$\approx 83.33\%$

Kimberly did best in Science.

9. ∠RQP = 180° − 125°
(pair of angles between 2 parallel sides = 180°)
$= 55°$
∠SQR = 55° − 32°
$= 23°$

10. ∠DEF = 180° − 155°
(pair of angles between 2 parallel sides = 180°)
$= 25°$
∠GFE = 180° − 117°
(pair of angles between 2 parallel sides = 180°)
$= 63°$

11. Total area of triangles ADX and CBY
$= \dfrac{1}{2}$ of area of rectangle ABCD
The diagonal AC splits XBYD into 2 halves.
$\dfrac{1}{4}$ of the rectangle is shaded.

12. ∠ABC = 60° (equilateral triangle)
∠BXZ = 180° − 60°
(pair of angles between 2 parallel sides = 180°)
$= 120°$
∠BXY = 120° − 28°
$= 92°$
∠BYX = 180° − 60° − 92°
(sum of angles in triangle)
$= 28°$

$\angle XYZ = (180° - 28°) \div 2$
    (base angles of isosceles triangle)
    $= 76°$
$\angle CYZ = 180° - 76° - 28°$
    (angles on a straight line)
    $= 76°$
$\angle YZC = 180° - 76° - 60°$
    (sum of angles in triangle)
    $= 44°$

Challenging Problems (pp. 146–151)

1. $180°$
2. 1
3. Every hour, the hour and minute hands form a right angle twice, except when they are between 2 to 4, and 8 to 10. So, in one day, the two hands form a right angle $(2 \times 24) - 4 = 44$ times.
4. Autumn: 3 h
   Diego: 2 h for $\frac{3}{4}$ of the journey
   Since Diego jogged $\frac{3}{4}$ of the journey in 2 h, he completed the whole journey in
   $2 \times \frac{4}{3} = \frac{8}{3}$ h.
   Autumn's time : Diego's time
   $=$ 3   : $\frac{8}{3}$
   $=$ 9   :   8
   The faster the speed, the shorter the time taken.
   Autumn's speed : Diego's speed = 8 : 9
   The ratio of Autumn's speed to Diego's is 8 : 9.
5. (a) 30 campers consume 40 kg of cereal in 14 days.
       35 campers consume 40 kg of cereal in $(14 \times 30) \div 35 = 12$ days.
       The same quantity of cereal will last for 12 days.
   (b) 30 campers consume 40 kg of cereal in 14 days.
       30 campers consume 60 kg in $(14 \times 60) \div 40 = 21$ days.
       The cereal will last for another $21 - 14 = 7$ days.
       The cereal will last for 7 more days.
6.   Van B   Van A
   120 km/h   100 km/h

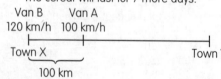

   Van B traveled $120 - 100 = 20$ km more in an hour than Van A.

Van A had already covered 100 km before Van B left Town X.
So, Van B would need $100 \div 20 = 5$ h to make up for the extra 100 km.
$5 \times 120 = 600$ km
The distance between the two towns was 600 km.

7. <u> 19 </u>   <u>   </u>   <u> 35 </u>   <u>   </u>   <u> 39 </u>
   The sum of the 5 numbers is $5 \times 30 = 150$.
   Since the range is 20, the 1st number is $39 - 20 = 19$.
   Since the median is 35, the sum of the 1st, 3rd, and 5th number is $19 + 35 + 39 = 93$.
   So the sum of the 2nd and 4th number is $150 - 93 = 57$.
   Greatest possible value for the 2nd number
   = 57 – least possible value for 4th number
   $= 57 - 36$
   $= 21$
   The greatest possible value for the second number is 21.

8.

<figure>

5

1

3   2

</figure>

    Unshaded : Shaded area : Unshaded
      area of   area of
      big circle   small circle
   $=$ 5   :   1
   $=$ 15   :   3
   $=$ 3   :   2
   In other words,
      Unshaded : Shaded area : Unshaded
      area of   area of
      big circle   small circle
   $=$ 15   :   3   :   2
   $\dfrac{3}{15 + 3 + 2} = \dfrac{3}{20}$
   $\dfrac{3}{20}$ of the figure is shaded.
9. Area of shaded part
   = Area of half of the rectangle – area of quarter circle
   Area of half of the rectangle
   $= \dfrac{1}{2} \times 30 \text{ cm} \times 20 \text{ cm}$
   $= 300 \text{ cm}^2$
   Radius of circle = 20 cm ÷ 2
                     = 10 cm

Area of quarter circle

$= \dfrac{1}{4} \times 3.14 \times 10 \text{ cm} \times 10 \text{ cm}$

$= 78.5 \text{ cm}^2$

Area of shaded part

$= 300 \text{ cm}^2 - 78.5 \text{ cm}^2$

$= 221.5 \text{ cm}^2$

The area of the shaded part is 221.5 cm^2.

10.

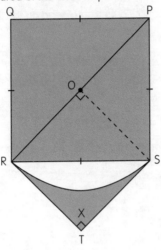

PR = 14 cm

Area of shaded square PQRS

$= 2 \times$ area of triangle PRS

$= 2 \times \dfrac{1}{2} \times PR \times OS$

$= 2 \times \dfrac{1}{2} \times 14 \text{ cm} \times (\dfrac{1}{2} \times 14 \text{ cm})$

$= 98 \text{ cm}^2$

Radius of quarter circle ORS $= \dfrac{1}{2} \times 14 \text{ cm}$

$= 7 \text{ cm}$

Area of quarter circle ORS

$= \dfrac{1}{4} \times \dfrac{22}{7} \times 7 \text{ cm} \times 7 \text{ cm}$

$= 38.5 \text{ cm}^2$

Area of small square ORTS $= 7 \text{ cm} \times 7 \text{ cm}$

$= 49 \text{ cm}^2$

Area of shaded part X

= Area of square ORTS – area of quarter circle ORS

$= 49 \text{ cm}^2 - 38.5 \text{ cm}^2$

$= 10.5 \text{ cm}^2$

Total area of shaded parts

$= 98 \text{ cm}^2 + 10.5 \text{ cm}^2$

$= 108.5 \text{ cm}^2$

The total area of the shaded parts is 108.5 cm^2.

12 Mixed Problems 3

Practice Questions (pp. 154–157)

1. $-83 + 47 = -36$

The diver is 36 ft. below the sea level.

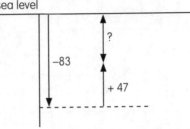

2.

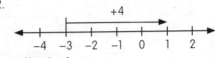

$(-3) + 4 = 1$

The temperature at 1:00 a.m. was 1°C.

3. The origin, O, indicates the main lobby.
The 3 changes are: (a) 5 floors up,
(b) 3 floors up, and
(c) 10 floors down.

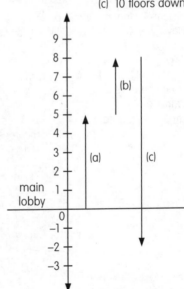

It is now 2 floors below the main lobby.

4. $8 \times 2250 + (3 \times -1750) = 18{,}000 - 5250$

$= 12{,}750$

Its final vertical height above sea leavel was 12,750 ft.

5. (a) $x = -1$

(b) $x = 2$

(c) $x = \dfrac{1}{2}$

6.

x	−2	−1	0	1	2
y	4	3	2	1	0

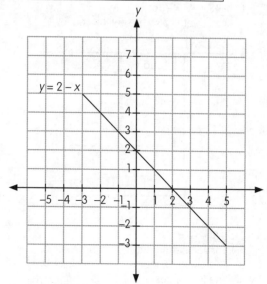

$y = 2 - x$

7. Probability that it will rain on
2 consecutive days
= Probability that it will rain on
Day 1 × Probability that it will rain on Day 2
= 0.3 × 0.3
= 0.09
The probability that it will rain on two
consecutive days in July is 0.09.

8. Method 1
Using a tree diagram

1st toss	2nd toss	3rd toss	Outcomes
		H	HHH
	H	T	HHT
H		H	HTH
	T	T	HTT
		H	THH
	H	T	THT
T		H	TTH
	T	T	TTT

Probability that Evan gets heads three times
$= \dfrac{1}{8}$
The probability that he gets heads three
times is $\dfrac{1}{8}$.

Method 2
Probability of getting a head on the 1st toss
$= \dfrac{1}{2}$
Probability of getting a head on the 2nd toss
$= \dfrac{2}{4}$
$= \dfrac{1}{2}$
Probability of getting a head on the 3rd toss
$= \dfrac{3}{6}$
$= \dfrac{1}{2}$
Probability that Evan gets heads three times
$= \dfrac{1}{2} \times \dfrac{1}{2} \times \dfrac{1}{2}$
$= \dfrac{1}{8}$
The probability that he gets heads three
times is $\dfrac{1}{8}$.

9. (a) $\dfrac{1}{8}$

(b) $\dfrac{1}{2}$

(c) $\dfrac{5}{8}$

10. $\dfrac{2}{3}$

Challenging Problems (pp. 159–164)

1. (a) greater; warmer
   (b) smaller; colder
   (c) colder; smaller
   (d) colder; smaller
   (e) warmer; greater
   (f) warmer; greater

2. (a) $[\dfrac{1}{5}y = -6 \div 3]$
   $\qquad = -2$
   $\dfrac{3}{5}y = -6$
   $y = -2 \times 5$
   $\quad = -10$

   (b) $q - 3 = -5$
   Adding 3 to both sides of the equation,
   we have
   $q - 3 + 3 = -5 + 3$
   $q = -2$

   (c) $2 - p = 5$
   Subtracting 2 from both sides of the
   equation, we have
   $2 - p - 2 = 5 - 2$
   $-p = 3$
   Multiply both sides of the equation by
   (−1), we have
   $-p \times (-1) = 3 \times (-1)$
   $p = -3$

(d) $3 - x = -5$

Subtract 3 from both sides of the equation, we have

$3 - x - 3 = -5 - 3$

$-x = -8$

Multiply both sides of the equation by (−1), we have

$-x \times (-1) = -8 \times (-1)$

$x = 8$

3.

Shoes	Socks	Combinations
Black	Black	Black shoes, black socks
	White	Black shoes, white socks
	Brown	Black shoes, brown socks
	Grey	Black shoes, grey socks
Red	Black	Red shoes, black socks
	White	Red shoes, white socks
	Brown	Red shoes, brown socks
	Grey	Red shoes, grey socks

(a) Probability of matching the black pair of shoes to the white or brown pair of socks

$= \dfrac{1}{8} + \dfrac{1}{8}$

$= \dfrac{1}{4}$

The probability of matching the black pair of shoes to the white or brown pair of socks is $\dfrac{1}{4}$.

(b) Probability of matching the black and red pair of shoes to the black or grey pair of socks

$= (\dfrac{1}{8} + \dfrac{1}{8}) + (\dfrac{1}{8} + \dfrac{1}{8})$

$= \dfrac{1}{2}$

The probability of matching the black and red pair of shoes to the black or grey pair of socks is $\dfrac{1}{2}$.

4. There are 10 consonants in the word. Probability that both cards show consonants

$= \dfrac{10}{15} \times \dfrac{9}{14}$

$= \dfrac{3}{7}$

The probability that both cards drawn show consonants is $\dfrac{3}{7}$.

5. Probability that he will get a 6 the first time

$= \dfrac{1}{6}$

Probability that he will get an odd number the second time $= \dfrac{3}{6}$

$= \dfrac{1}{2}$

Probability that he will get a 6 the first time and an odd number the second time

$= \dfrac{1}{6} \times \dfrac{1}{2}$

$= \dfrac{1}{12}$

The probability that he will get a 6 the first time and an odd number the second time is $\dfrac{1}{12}$.

6. (a) $\dfrac{3}{6} = \dfrac{1}{2}$

(b) $\dfrac{1}{6} \times \dfrac{3}{5} = \dfrac{1}{10}$

(c) $\dfrac{3}{6} \times \dfrac{2}{5} = \dfrac{1}{5}$

7.

+	1	2	3	4	5	6
1	2	3	4	⑤	6	7
2	3	4	⑤	6	7	8
3	4	⑤	6	7	8	9
4	⑤	6	7	8	9	⑩
5	6	7	8	9	⑩	11
6	7	8	9	⑩	11	12

From the possibility diagram, the total number of possible outcomes is 36.

Number of outcomes where the sum of the scores is a multiple of 5 = 7

The probability that the sum of the scores on the dice is a multiple of 5 is $\dfrac{7}{36}$.

8. Probability of picking a U.S. stamp $= \dfrac{1}{3}$

Probability of picking a Singapore stamp

$= \dfrac{2}{9}$

Probability of picking a U.S. or Singapore stamp $= \dfrac{1}{3} + \dfrac{2}{9}$

$= \dfrac{5}{9}$

Probability of picking a China stamp

$= 1 - \dfrac{5}{9}$

$= \dfrac{4}{9}$

$\dfrac{4}{9} \longrightarrow 12$

$\dfrac{1}{9} \longrightarrow 12 \div 4 = 3$

$\dfrac{9}{9} \longrightarrow 9 \times 3 = 27$

There are 27 stamps in the envelope.

9. (a) Since the fractional parts must add up to 1, the cylinders are $1 - \frac{1}{2} - \frac{1}{3} = \frac{1}{6}$ of the set of blocks.

   If $\frac{1}{6}$ of the set represents 9 blocks,

   then there are $9 \times 6 = 54$ blocks.

   (b) There are $\frac{1}{2} \times 54 = 27$ pyramids in the box.

   (c) There are $\frac{1}{3} \times 54 = 18$ rectangular prisms in the box.

10. (a)

Coin	Spinner	Combination
	1	H1
	2	H2
Head	3	H3
	4	H4
	5	H5
	1	T1
	2	T2
Tail	3	T3
	4	T4
	5	T5

   There are 10 possible outcomes.

   (b) (i) The theoretical probability of getting a tail and a 5 is $\frac{1}{10}$.

   (ii) The theoretical probability of getting a head and a 0 is 0.

   (iii) The theoretical probability of getting a tail and an odd number is $\frac{3}{10}$.

   (iv) The theoretical probability of getting a head and an even number is $\frac{1}{5}$.